# The Technique of
# Landscape Painting

# The Technique of
# Landscape Painting

by Frederic Taubes

Watson-Guptill Publications / *New York*

*Other Books by Frederic Taubes*

Oil Painting for the Beginner

The Painter's Question and Answer Book

Painting Materials and Techniques

Pen and Ink Drawing

Modern Art: Sweet or Sour

Painting Techniques, Ancient and Modern

The Quickest Way to Paint Well

Better Frames for Your Pictures

The Mastery of Oil Painting

Pictorial Anatomy of the Human Body

The Technique of Oil Painting

You Don't Know What You Like

Studio Secrets

The Amateur Painter's Handbook

Anatomy of Genius

Pictorial Composition and the Art of Drawing

Taubes' Paintings and Essays on Art

New Essays on Art

Illustrated Guide to the Great Art of Europe

The Art and Technique of Portrait Painting

New Techniques in Painting

Abracadabra and Modern Art

The Quickest Way to Draw Well

# Contents

page 13   FOREWORD

page 15   1. PAINTING TOOLS
    15  Tools
    15  Bristle Brushes
    17  Flat Sable Brushes
    17  Round Sable Brushes
    18  Scriptliner
    19  Striper
    21  Care of Brushes
    22  Painting Knives
    22  Faults of Knives
    22  Good Knives
    23  Conditioning Knives
    24  Value of Painting Knives

page 25   2. CANVAS, PANELS, AND MISCELLANEOUS SUPPLIES
    25  Canvas
    25  Comparing Canvas Samples
    27  Preparing Your Own Canvas
    28  Acrylic Gesso
    28  Preparing A Panel
    28  Advantages and Disadvantages of Panels
    29  Miscellaneous Materials

*page 30*  3. COLORS

30  Complete List of Colors
31  Flake White
31  Ivory Black and Mars Black
31  Prussian Blue
31  Phthalo Blue
32  Ultramarine Blue
32  Viridian Green
32  Phthalo Green
32  Chrome Oxide Green Dull
32  Naples Yellow
32  Yellow Ochre
33  Brown Ochre
33  Mars Yellow
33  Raw Siena
33  Strontium and Zinc Yellows
33  Cadmium Yellow Light, Medium, and
     Cadmium Orange
33  Hansa Yellow
33  Cadmium Red Light
34  Alizarin Crimson
34  Venetian Red
34  Mars Violet
34  Burnt Siena
34  Umber, Burnt and Raw
34  Mars Brown
34  Principal Characteristics of Colors


*page 35*  4. PAINT DILUENTS

35  Short Paint vs. Long
36  Function of Painting Media
37  Soft and Hard Resins
37  Copal Painting Media
41  Other Diluents and Liquids


*page 42*  5. PICTORIAL COMPOSITION

42  Problems of Composition
43  Nature of Composition
48  Strategy of Composition
48  Coherence, Unity, Emphasis
50  Characteristics of Compositions


*page 58*  6. PERSPECTIVE, PICTURE FORMAT,
           LIGHT AND SHADE

58  Foreground, Middleground, Background
59  History of Perspective

63 Sharp Focus—Soft Focus
64 Atmospheric Perspective
64 Color Balance
65 Picture Format
66 Division of Pictorial Space
68 Light and Shade
68 Dispersed Light
68 Focal Light

*page 70* **7. COLOR MIXING**

70 Characteristics of Color Mixtures
73 Color Mixtures for Specific Purposes
73 Clear Skies
73 Clouds
74 The Horizon
74 Middleground and Foreground
74 Classical and other Systems
75 Trees
75 Rocks
75 Water
76 General Observations

*page 77* **8. GLAZES AND SCUMBLES**

77 Glazing
80 Hard Resins in Glazes
80 Scumbling
80 Three Kinds of Scumbles

*page 82* **9. ALLA PRIMA PAINTING**

82 History of Alla Prima Technique
83 Characteristics of the Technique
83 First Step—Drawing
83 Second Step—Imprimatura
84 Third Step—Glazing
85 Completing the Painting
89 Varnishing and Corrections
89 Multicolored Imprimatura
89 Alla Prima Painting on Toned Ground
89 Step-by-step Procedure
92 Open Color Painting

*page 95* **10. PAINTING ON A UNDERPAINTING**

96 Underpainting in Stages
97 Six Basic Recommendations
97 General Observations
97 A Brief History of Classic Techniques

*98* Color in Underpainting
*98* Color Mixtures Used in Underpainting


*page 100* 11. SKIES, TREES, ROCKS, WATER

*100* Skies
*101* Painting Trees
*108* Painting Trees: Demonstration 1
*112* Painting Trees: Demonstration 2
*112* Painting A Forest
*118* Painting Rocks: Demonstration 1
*118* Painting Rocks: Demonstration 2
*119* Painting Rocks: Demonstration 3
*119* Painting Rocks: Demonstration 4
*119* Rock Colors
*123* Painting Water
*127* Further Observations


*page 135* 12. THE ART OF LANDSCAPE PAINTING

*135* Gathering Pictorial Material
*136* Classic Principles of Landscape Construction
*137* Demonstration of Classic Technique: Underpainting
*140* Demonstration of Classic Technique: Final Painting


*page 141* 13. VARNISHING

*141* How Varnish Protects Paintings
*142* Recommended Varnishes
*142* Miscellaneous Comments on Varnishing


*page 144* 14. ANALYSES OF LANDSCAPE PAINTING

*144* Studying Old Masters
*162* 19th Century Paintings


*page 169* GLOSSARY


*page 171* INDEX

# The Technique of
# Landscape Painting

# Foreword

Through the years I have written many books on art techniques. You may well ask, what distinguishes the present volume from all the others? More far reaching and deeper experience. Over thirty years of work with students of all categories—beginners as well as accomplished artists—taught me a lesson, or more accurately, perfected my approach to things pictorial. This experience has allowed me to make my presentation more precise and practical. In short, this book contains the quintessence of my experiences as a landscape painter.

F.T.
*New York, 1966*

# CHAPTER 1

# *Painting tools*

Is any special equipment required in painting landscapes? Yes, the endless number and diversity of motifs that face the landscape painter will call for a wider array of tools and colors than are required, for example, in portrait painting. Some may say that two brushes and five colors could produce a masterpiece; they might argue that, with a minimum of equipment, one could paint any type of landscape with dispatch. No doubt, this is true. With equal justification, one could maintain that the most elaborate equipment may fail to aid the artist in performing his task.

All tools used by the artist can aid him in his craftsmanship. Craftsmanship can be simple, elaborate, or extremely complex, depending on the performer's propensities and idiosyncrasies. Those who are fascinated by the challenge of craftsmanship will not deny themselves the opportunity to employ all the useful tools and colors at their disposal.

## TOOLS

In regard to painting, the term, *tool*, applies to two categories: brushes and painting knives. These are the means by which paint can be transferred to a support. Of course, the character of this transfer will differ with the character of the particular tool. Moreover, the tools you select can make the very act of painting easy, difficult, or, in some instances, altogether impossible.

## BRISTLE BRUSHES

These are the first brushes the painter thinks of, although, as you will see later, they share their importance equally with sable brushes and knives. Bristle brushes are available in two categories: *flats* and *brights*. The flats have long bristles; the brights, short.

The short ones, being less elastic, are more suitable for underpainting and for initial work, where fluid brushstrokes are not important. When brights are used for final painting, they leave harsh marks which may be undesirable, especially when these marks extend over the entire picture surface, thus producing monotonous textures.

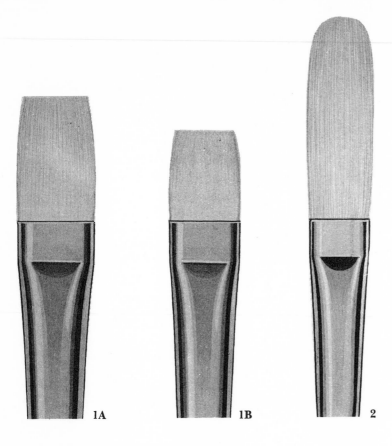

Figure 1A This brush is called *flat*: it has long bristles, hence produces fluent strokes. 1B The short bristles account for the relative stiffness of the head of bristles, which makes this brush, called *bright,* suitable for a more vigorous workout.

Figure 2 An extra long head of bristles is useful for large pictures where great fluency of brushstrokes is desirable.

For the later stages of a painting—in which fluid brushstrokes are more important—the elastic flats and sables are more suitable.

In some of the earlier, academic schools which stressed energetic, vigorous brushwork, brights were the painter's mainstay. The prototype of energetic brushwork can be found in the work of Frans Hals, whom many followers of the academic school tried to emulate. However, Hals used bristle brushes quite different from our own. The bristle brushes used before the invention of the metallic ferrule (at the beginning of the 19th century) were oval; hence, the texture left by these earlier brushes is not identical with the texture produced by our modern brushes.

Of course, it is not only the character of a brush which determines the particular texture of the paint body. The nature of paint itself will, in large measure, create a particular surface effect. (The texture of the paint body and the nature of paint will be dealt with in later chapters.)

There is also another category of bristle brushes, one having a round ferrule, commonly called a round bristle brush. Such brushes do not have the required working quality, especially when the head of bristles is too short. If the thickness of the body of bristles is correctly related to their length—to provide proper flexibility—some may find round bristle brushes to their liking.

Lastly, a brush with an extra long body of bristles, and hence having great elasticity, can be useful when you paint on larger surfaces (see Fig. 2).

Now, two considerations should be kept in mind when you buy bristle brushes: quality and size. As to quality, it is always prudent to buy the best; a well made brush will not only outlast two inferior ones, but its working properties will be vastly superior. In a superior brush, the bristles bend from both ends toward the middle (a type known as *toed-in* or *interlocked* bristles); this design allows the body of the bristles to remain in a compact shape. Moreover, such brushes are made of the best quality bristles. Inferior brushes quickly lose their com-

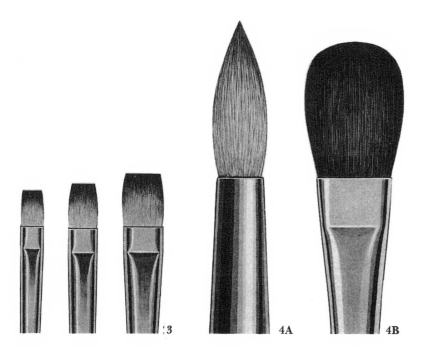

Figure 3 Flat sable brushes are used for producing soft textures and for blending colors.

Figure 4A An extra large, round, soft-hair brush, often referred to as Sabeline, is essential in instances when our largest round sable brush (No. 8) appears to be too small. 4B This soft hair brush, usually made of squirrel hair, serves for delicate blending of colors. Such brushes are either oval or square.

pactness and become scraggy.

A range of brushes between numbers 3 and 10 will encompass the entire array of useful tools. The largest brush, number 12, could be used only on large surfaces, such as 40" x 50". In average size paintings, the most frequently used brushes are numbers 4, 5, and 7.

#### FLAT SABLE BRUSHES

The flat and the round sable brush are distinctly different tools. The flat brush operates like the bristle brush, except that its soft hair does not leave the same strong marks in the body of paint (Fig. 3). Thus, this brush is a weak tool, chiefly effective for delicate blending of colors or for producing smooth surfaces. For small paintings treated in a miniaturistic manner, such a brush is most satisfactory. Of course, the support used, in this instance, must be almost without texture. The useful size of flat sables ranges from ⅛" to 1" wide.

Sable hair brushes are expensive. Cheaper brushes are made of oxhair, but their strokes are not as soft. Large, flat and round brushes are made of a sable hair substitute called *Sabeline*. Flat brushes made of squirrel hair are used only for blending; Sabelines are usually about 1" wide and are therefore suitable for blending larger areas. In fact, one could consider them indispensable for this purpose (Fig. 4).

#### ROUND SABLE BRUSHES

This brush is generally considered useful *only* in watercolor painting, because the soft hairs will not properly distribute paint of "normal" consistency (as it comes from the tube). However, the round sable is extremely valuable in oil painting if used with paint *thinned by the medium*. In the classic technique discussed in this book, practically all paint requires thinning by the medium; therefore, you will need round sables whenever you paint (Fig. 5).

The standard watercolor brush comes in sizes from number oo to 12, although this numbering is not used by all manufacturers. When you paint small landscapes, numbers 1 to 5 do well;

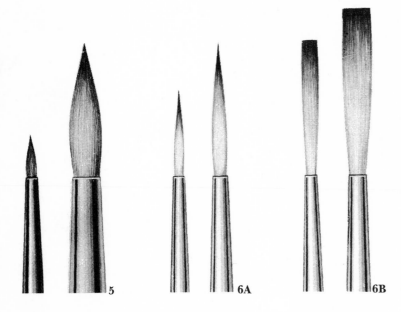

Figure 5  Standard round sable brushes.

Figure 6A  The scriptliner is available in various thicknesses and lengths. The longer the body of hair, the more liquid paint it can take on. The extra long sable hairs do not allow execution of precise miniaturistic details. 6B The striper differs from the scriptliner in that its body of hair terminates in a flat chisel-like shape. Hence, the strokes made with it are wide and powerful.

for larger paintings, numbers 8 to 12 may be used.

What is the particular character of the round sable brush? Its working quality is that of a drawing tool. While your hand must be *conditioned* to the particular manipulation which the shape of the *bristle* brush dictates, the *round* sable brush is like a pencil or pen with which we have been familiar since childhood. This does not imply that a round sable is suitable only for linear effects, or for details. In fact, you can employ it as well for broad, pictorial demarcations; in certain cases, it may eliminate our old standby, the bristle brush. Of course, a round sable brush is totally unsuitable for underpainting.

### SCRIPTLINER

This very special instrument is still a stranger in most artists' studios (Fig. 6A). To my knowledge, its uses were first described in one of my earlier books. Its marks are so characteristic that they may be verified in some of the old masters'

works, especially in canvases by Guardi, Canaletto, and Tiepolo, where its use is always evident.

Now, what makes this tool so valuable—I would say indispensable—in landscape painting? It is the capacity to produce fine, coherent, or staccato lines over relatively large areas without frequent reloading. Because of the length of its body of sables, the scriptliner can store a lot of *very thin* paint. The thinness of the paint is essential, for the highly flexible sables are incapable of moving stiff paint. In fact, oil colors thinned to the consistency of watercolor by Copal Painting Medium are most appropriate for this purpose. Paint of extra long (fluid) consistency, conditioned by Copal Concentrate, can be used very effectively with this brush.

Why do I emphasize the need for copal resin in connection with extra thin paint? Thin paint will not attach itself firmly to the support (canvas or panel placed in an upright position) unless the painting medium contains a resin. Now, since a soft resin, such as damar or mastic, must

Figure 7A *Coast Landscape*
(26 x 40). Horizontal lines, made
chiefly with stripers, are evident
throughout the picture. A
scriptliner was used only for
smaller details.

Figure 7B Detail of upper left
hand corner, showing use of
scriptliner.

19

8A

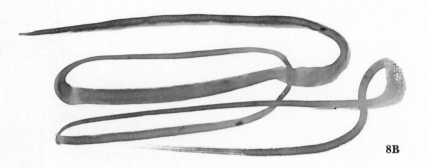

8B

Figure 8 Marks produced by the scriptliner (8A) and the striper (8B). The brushes were dipped only once in a pool of liquid paint; therefore the delineations show no interruption.

not be used for permanent painting, the old standby, copal, seems the only logical choice.

What are the *limitations* of this brush? If you want a very precise stroke—as in placing a highlight on a pupil or delineating eyelashes—the scriptliner is not the most efficient tool. Here the standard number 3 round sable brush will be more satisfactory. However, in landscape painting, I can think of only rare occasions when (on small surfaces, 8″ x 10″ or smaller) you would need such an ultra-precise demarcation. Of course, for miniaturistic details, the round, small sable brush will prove best.

What is the nature of the strokes produced by the scriptliner? They can register every nervous impulse of the artist's fingers more effectively than any other instrument. Even dormant or inhibited impulses of the hand seem to be miraculously liberated by this brush.

## STRIPER

The striper, as its name indicates, is capable

of producing stripes, lines of appreciable width (Fig. 6B). Whereas the scriptliner terminates in a sharp point, the tip of the striper is chisel shaped. This property permits more vigorous strokes, linear effects of great authority.

Like the scriptliner, this brush can hold large quantities of liquid paint. This is an enormous advantage in sustaining the original impulses of your hand. When you move your brush away from the canvas to take on fresh paint (your most frequent movement with a conventional brush), your original impulse is interrupted, and sometimes even stopped. This accounts for the often mechanical look of paintings which rely on precise manipulation of the brush.

Marks produced with the scriptliner and the striper are seen in Fig. 8. In Fig. 7 (and Fig. 7B), *Low Tide* (28″ x 40″), you can see ample use of both the scriptliner and striper; in fact, their lines form the framework of the entire picture.

## CARE OF BRUSHES

When well treated, brushes of good quality have

20

considerable longevity. Good treatment calls for washing the brush with soap and water after use, and taking special care to eliminate all paint residue from the neck of the ferrule, where trouble usually starts. Washing in turpentine is not enough; soap is *essential* to wash away linseed oil and pigment particles.

Some people prefer to clean brushes in a petroleum derivative (like kerosene) and leave them submerged in the solvent for use the next day. There is no objection to such treatment, except that you must dry the brushes well before you start painting again. If not, the solvent will adhere to the brush, and will thin both paint and medium, which is disadvantageous to both. Another disadvantage is that such treatment does not allow you to shape the heads of bristles and sables to their proper configuration, which is particularly important in maintaining good working quality of sable brushes.

A bristle brush, if not the best, tends to spread out after some use. If the bristles are long enough, you can prevent spreading if you wrap soft paper around the head of bristles after washing, so they will taper toward the end. However, a fuzzy brush does not necessarily become useless, because there may be times when you want to produce fuzzy effects. Flat sable brushes should be treated in the same way. But the round sable brush and the script-liner should be brought to a perfect point after washing. This is best done by shaping them between your lips.

Once any brush loses its shape because of wear, it can still be saved. Up to ½″ can often be added to its length, as shown in Fig. 9. This is done in the following manner. Notch the flattened (or round) ferrule with a three-cornered file and cut it through in one spot. Bend and twist the marked portion of the ferrule back and forth with pliers until the metal breaks open. Then take hold of the end piece of the metal (on the edge previously cut open) with the pliers and peel it off. You can also perform this operation with metal shears, or even with strong surgical shears. If the entire flattened part of the ferrule has been cut off, the round portion should be flattened with a hammer. The uncovered bristle or sable hair must now be soft-

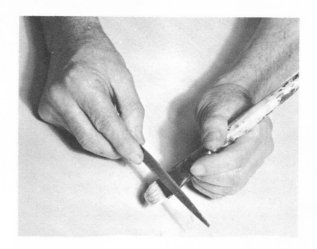

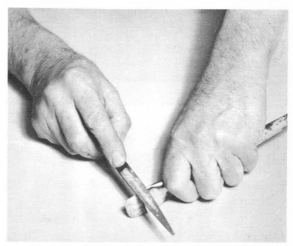

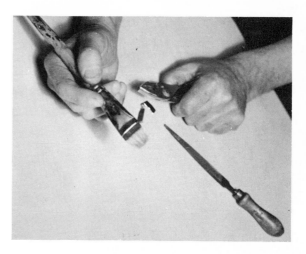

Figure 9 Adding length to worn out brushes. The same operation can be performed on a flat or round sable brush. 9A Notching the wide side of the ferrule with a file. 9B Filing down the narrow side of the ferrule. 9C Peeling off the cut portion of the ferrule.

21

ened by a strong solvent (such as commercial paint remover) which will remove the plastic adhesive which holds the hair at the neck of the ferrule; this will also dissolve dried paint.

Brushes hardened by dried paint or varnish should be submerged in paint remover, which softens the residue quickly and thoroughly. There is no proof that paint remover, which usually combines acetone with alcohol and paraffin, harms bristle or sable brushes. Once dried paint sticks to the neck of the ferrule, paint will continue to accumulate. Only paint remover will successfully eliminate this residue.

An inelastic head of bristles, one that is too short and stubby, will prove entirely useless. A head of bristles too long and thin will be too weak to distribute paint, although such brushes could be used to blend colors. Of course, once a brush starts to shed hair, you should discard it. All this is equally true of bristle and sable brushes.

### PAINTING KNIVES

Painting knives, habitually called *palette knives* (perhaps because they are sometimes used to scrape paint from the palette), are painting tools just as important as brushes. Whereas a brush seems a "basic" instrument, one should acquire a taste for palette knives as well. The painting knife is not as popular as it should be because it can be completely useless unless it possesses certain definite qualities.

### FAULTS OF KNIVES

Let us take a look at the really useless tool which has discouraged so many painters. Typically, its blade is too short, too long, or too stiff. Thus, your hand must exert too much pressure on the canvas. This increased pressure has two disadvantages: first, it impedes the swift and delicate operation of your hand; second, too much pressure will squeeze the paint from under the knife blade, preventing the efficient distribution of the paint. A blade that is too elastic will also fail to distribute the paint properly, although a very elastic blade has its use, to which I shall refer later. Further, blades that

are too wide or too narrow (in relation to their length) are deficient. A blade that bends away right at the neck of the handle is useless; the same can be said of a blade that is equally thick in its entire length.

Then, sometimes the handle itself is poorly shaped so that it lies awkwardly in your hand. Japanese knives possess superbly shaped handles, and have balanced relationships between handle and blade.

There is another category of painting knives: ones with small, trowel-shaped, very elastic, often fancifully designed blades (Fig. 10). These, in my opinion, are totally inadequate instruments; they force your hand to work indirectly over a "gear"—the bend of the trowel—rather than allow your fingers' impulses to be transmitted directly to the support. Your fingers *should feel* the action of the blade directly; a straight knife works like an extension of your finger, operating directly on the painting surface. Nevertheless, the trowel-shaped instrument is widely used, presumably because of its intriguing look, and it may be adequate for the limited requirements of some.

### GOOD KNIVES

It is obvious that words cannot explain the degree of elasticity necessary for the blade in relation to its length. However, the correct proportions of blades are given in the drawings below. Basically, you need three categories of knives: for underpainting, for painting, and for blending paint.

In underpainting, you must exert pressure on the canvas to force stiff paint into the fabric; thus, an underpainting knife must be stiffer than the one used for overpainting.

The interstices (the spaces between the fibers) of a canvas cannot be filled by a brush. And why is it imperative to reduce the original tooth (roughness) of the canvas? Simply because a brushstroke, even one made with a bristle brush, will not register well on such a surface; a sable brush cannot operate on it at all. Of course, we are dealing here with a normal canvas support, that is, one possessing appreciable tooth.

Although I call it an *underpainting* knife,

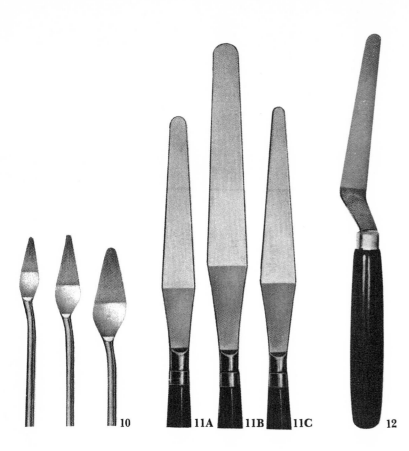

Figure 10 Blades of common spatulas, essentially ineffective.

Figure 11 Properly constructed painting knives. 11A Underpainting knife. To perform its task, this instrument must have a blade sufficiently strong to press the paint material into the interstices of the canvas, yet elastic enough to deposit the paint without undue pressure. 11B The length and elasticity of this knife allows it to be used for blending paint and also for underpainting large surfaces. 11C The painting knife, with its tapering elastic blade, allows all necessary painting operations assigned to it.

Figure 12 A spatula is used for various purposes, depending on the size and elasticity of the blade. Stiff blades are well suited for mixing dry pigment with oil, and for scraping dry paint from the palette. Large, more elastic blades can be used to size and prime raw fabric.

this does not mean that underpainting *must* be done with a knife; it can be done throughout with a brush. But afterwards, use the knife to smooth out the texture and to force the paint into the weave of the fabric. On large canvases, where small details are not considered, you can underpaint the *entire surface* with the knife.

There is also a small knife (Fig. 11A) which can handle small details. Its blade tapers off to a narrow point, and it is more flexible at its tip than at the handle end. The end of this blade is also stiffer than that used for general painting.

The second *basic knife* (Fig. 11B) is used for painting proper, that is, after the underpainting is done. The blade of this most sensitive instrument should have just the right properties to create any desired effect, such as impasti (thick applications of paint), or the thinnest glazes (transparent films of color). Only large areas cannot be blended very well with this tool.

The third knife (Fig. 11C) is ideally suited for blending because of its long blade, 4″ of which will touch the canvas without your exerting too much pressure. Again, I should empha-

size that when you bear down on the blade with any degree of pressure, the paint will smear, but not blend. You can also use this knife to smooth any undesirable roughness of the underpainting, as long as the paint is still wet.

An instrument useful for various purposes, such as sizing and priming canvases, is seen in Fig. 12. This knife is also practical for mixing dry pigment with linseed oil (in preparing one's own paint material).

### CONDITIONING KNIVES

The elasticity or stiffness of blades depends on the metal's thickness. A blade which is too thin cannot be improved; but thick blades can be made more elastic by grinding them down on a grinding stone. Electric grinders, however, are not suitable because the rapidly rotating stone may burn the metal, and does not allow proper control. Hence, you should use stones either moved by hand or by slowly moving gears. The shape of a blade can also be changed by cutting it in any metalworking shop.

23

Through use, blades wear out and their edges often get razor-sharp. To reduce this sharpness, rotate the blade in an upright position on carborundum paper to blunt the edge. With the carborundum paper, you can remove the burr that forms on the edges. If you continue to use such a blade, it will lose some of the metal from its working edges. When the blade loses its straight edge in this way, use a flat file to restore the blade's original condition: move the knife edge back and forth against the stationary file.

If knives are not used even for long intervals, they need not be protected against rust; traces of oil always cling to them and tend to prevent corrosion.

Important: *the blade of a painting knife must always be completely free of dried paint or imperfections of any kind;* these will always mar the paint film when the knife is used.

The blades of knives are vulnerable; they should be used only for indicated purposes. Do not give in to the temptation to scrape dried paint from the palette with the painting instrument. This is a frequent error of inexperienced painters. For scraping paint, use the knife shown in Fig. 12.

### VALUE OF PAINTING KNIVES

My careful discussion of painting knives shows my predilection for this instrument. Experience has shown that, when skillfully used, a painting knife may eliminate the need for any other tool except the round sable brush. This means that practically any painting can be fully realized when it is worked out with an array of proper knives and sable brushes, including a scriptliner. The general rule is: use knives for vigorous work and for broad effects; reserve delicate brushes for details and for delineation.

The painting knife is hardly a modern tool. It was always used for the preparation of canvas; the surfaces of old masters' paintings, from the 16th century on, point unmistakably to this fact (earlier paintings were generally done on wood panels). For the achievement of final effects, however, you can see its use on canvases from the 17th century on.

Why do I always refer to canvases? Because the knife does not operate well on rigid surfaces (panels), since such surfaces do not respond to the movements of the blade. In other words, when you strike a surface with a blade, the instrument and the support should *give* and *take;* there is no give in a rigid surface. Hence, the use of a knife on a panel is limited. But, a skillful hand, using a blade of proper flexibility, can create sensitive textures even on a rigid surface.

# CHAPTER 2

# Canvas, panels, and miscellaneous supplies

The term *support* refers to the surface you paint on, regardless of its nature. Strangely, not only amateur painters, but even seasoned practitioners often give little attention to the physical properties of the material upon which they paint. The reason for this neglect is that problems of craftsmanship, and hence concern with paint quality, have fallen to a state of low esteem. Paint quality—which combines texture, brushstroke, and treatment of contours—is strongly conditioned by the character of the support.

**CANVAS**

Canvas, the most widely used material, will receive our first consideration. There are two general types: linen and cotton. What is the difference between these? Between fabrics of equal weight, linen has greater tensile strength; however, a heavier cotton fabric will be *stronger* than a lighter linen material. Also linen fiber is often more hygroscopic than cotton; that is, linen reacts more to atmospheric humidity.

However, these characteristics are not our primary concern. Our chief consideration is the nature of the fabric's texture. In cotton canvas, this texture always has an even, mechanical quality; hence, it lacks the inherent sensitivities of a linen weave. Of course, there are also types of linen which are smooth and regular; yet even this refined condition is much more pleasing to the eye in linen than in cotton. The more you familiarize yourself with these qualities, the more you will recognize these conditions. To take an extreme example, compare slick kitchen oil cloth with a hand loomed textile.

**COMPARING CANVAS SAMPLES**

Four kinds of fabrics are reproduced in Fig. 13. They range from the smoothest to the roughest canvas offered in the trade.

There is still smoother canvas to be had, which resembles kitchen oil cloth. It is made of cotton and is completely toothless; its surface shows no visible grain. Can such a surface be

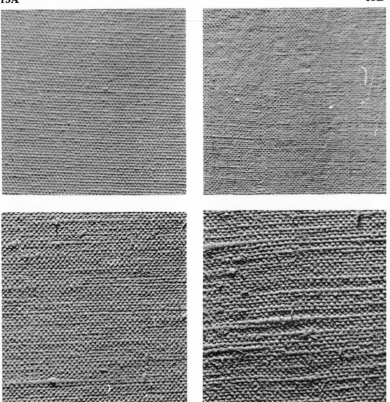

**13A**  **13B**

**13C**  **13D**

Figure 13    Four kinds of canvas used by the painter. 13A. The standard cotton fabric is single primed; its grain is unattractive. It should receive a second priming. 13B A fine linen material, single primed, with little tooth left; excellent for small paintings, also for alla prima work on toned ground. 13C A medium rough fabric, double primed, suitable for any size larger than 12″ x 16″. 13D The strongest of all the linen materials available for painting. Because of its overprominent grain and the hard quality of its threads, it is not agreeable for use in normally proportioned pictures; but it is best for mural painting, when it is triple primed and pasted on walls.

used successfully for fine art painting? I doubt it, because its blank smoothness lacks anything that would attract the eye. Can such a surface be underpainted and then gone over with a knife? Hardly; for the knife to operate well, there must be sufficient interstices left between the fibers, into which the knife can literally push the paint. Can you paint on such a surface with impasto (thick paint)? Not very well, for an appreciable mass of paint would not find sufficient anchorage on the toothless surface; hence the stability of such a thick paint film would be impaired. And how about alla prima work? You could do this very well on such a smooth surface, but here again, the largely transparent paint application would reveal the unattractive foundation beneath.

Fig. 13A depicts the most widely used cotton fabric. This one is single primed, which usually means that only one layer of priming was applied on top of the sized surface. (Sizing means covering the raw fabric with a glue solution; this layer of glue is followed by one or more layers of white paint, usually white lead, called

the *priming*.) To prepare this fabric for painting, you must use a good quantity of paint in the underpainting and use a painting knife to press the paint into the interstices. Thus, you will substantially reduce the tooth of the fabric. Why is this so important? Simply because a rough surface *swallows up the brushstrokes,* or at least impedes the movement of the brush. Of course, fine sable brush marks would fail to register on such a surface altogether.

The second example, Fig. 13B, shows a very fine linen fabric. This one is also single primed, but here a double priming (customary on coarser surfaces) would deprive it of its tooth. Even the underpainting must be done very thinly in this instance. Altogether, such fine fabrics are suitable only for small or medium sized pictures, ranging to about 16″ x 20″. You should keep in mind that the weight of a canvas must always relate to the picture's size. This fine linen, if double primed, can serve for alla prima technique (see Chapter 9).

The third canvas, Fig. 13C, is of average texture—neither too smooth nor too coarse—

whether single or double primed. It can be used very well for sizes to about 25″ x 30″, or even considerably larger. However, for a size of 30″ x 36″, I would choose the canvas in Fig. 13D. Even three thin primings would not deprive *this* linen of its tooth.

Lastly, there is an extra heavy linen of great toughness on the market. However, because of its prominent grain, this type of linen is not desirable; even high impasto does not look well on it.

### PREPARING YOUR OWN CANVAS

Thus far, I have referred to material bought ready-made in art supply stores. But nowadays many stores carry raw linen for those who prefer to prepare canvases themselves. What are the advantages of this material? There is only one, but it is important enough to lead you to consider the preparation of your own canvas: when a piece of linen (not cotton) is stretched on wooden stretchers and thus pulled in all directions, the woof and the warp of the fabric become variegated, giving it a *hand made* appearance. In other words, you thus overcome the mechanical aspect of the commercially manufactured canvas. Moreover, I might add, the price of the home prepared canvas is considerably lower, and the price becomes really negligible if cotton fabric is used.

Sizing and priming canvas are simple and easy tasks. First, stretch the raw material taut on the stretchers. Then size it; that is, cover it with a solution of glue. Use the best quality carpenter or rabbit skin glue in a 7% solution (one ounce of glue to one ounce of water). Only this kind of glue will gel at normal room temperature. Inferior material may not gel even at temperatures of 50° F., which will show that its adhesive properties are poor.

Why do we require a gel for sizing, rather than the liquid solution? In liquid state, the size would soak through the fabric and would fail to clog its interstices, thus allowing the priming solution to penetrate to the reverse side of the fabric, a condition which entails many disadvantages.

The gel should be sufficiently firm to turn to mush when crushed with the spatula; the gel must not become liquid again—an indication that its quality is inferior. Spread the glue-mush thinly on the canvas with the spatula. This done, leave the canvas to dry at normal room temperature. Exposure to heat (to accelerate its drying) would burst the fine membrane of size and thus defeat our main purpose, which is to seal off the top surface of the canvas.

To prevent fraying of the material around the outer edges of the stretchers, it is advisable to cover these edges with the liquefied glue. Thus prepared, the canvas will be dry in an hour or two.

After it dries, sand the sized surface. This operation usually removes the size from some of the top grain of the fabric. Hence, a second application of size should follow. It is best to start spreading the gel in the middle of the canvas which causes the fabric to contract, and allows you to cover the surface directly over the stretcher bars. Be sure the canvas is sufficiently taut; or protect it by inserting a cardboard between stretcher bar and canvas. *Otherwise, marks will form along the inside edges of the bars, causing the gel to penetrate to the reverse side.* Once this happens, the unsightly lines will show up through the priming on the finished painting.

White lead is the material traditionally used for priming; the commercial grade sold under the trade name, Dutch Boy (*in paste,* not in liquid form), is not only the best for this purpose, but the cheapest as well. When I say the best, I mean that it is the densest of all the white lead materials available because it is compounded with the least amount of oil. Except in priming, this paint is not suitable for artistic purposes inasmuch as it gradually turns yellow upon drying.

When used for priming or even for underpainting, however, this change is not significant. The canned paste is usually too stiff to be moved easily by the spatula; in this instance, thin it with Copal Painting Medium Light and use the trowel-shaped instrument for priming. Again, it is good practice *to insert a cardboard between the stretcher and the canvas* so you do not make marks along the stretcher edge.

The procedure I have just described, used since the 15th century, is simple enough. But for those who find it too cumbersome, I can recommend a more modern method of priming. This newer one employs an acrylic polymer emulsion, such as Liquitex Gesso, which has many advantages: it dries fast, provides an excellent surface for oil painting, and, unlike glue size, is not subject to mold. There is, however, one disadvantage in using this material on canvas. Should a bulge develop by accident (usually pressure against the canvas, a frequent occurrence when paintings are moved around), the acrylic emulsion, being water-insoluble, cannot be repaired in the same way as the traditionally sized surface.

Priming and sizing with acrylic polymer emulsion are done (simultaneously) in the following manner. Slightly dip a common utility brush in the undiluted acrylic gesso and go over the canvas *lightly*. Should you drench the canvas, the emulsion would penetrate the reverse side, and thus stiffen the canvas. The second priming can then be done with the spatula, which will move the liquid material very easily, depositing it in the interstices of the canvas. Both these applications can be done in less that half an hour; within one hour, work can proceed on such a priming. The acrylic gesso is quite flexible; hence as many applications can be carried out as required.

### PREPARING A PANEL

First let us look at panels from a historic perspective. Traditionally, when the art of painting started to develop (or more accurately, to assert itself again, for painting had been done in antiquity), from the 13th century on, only wooden panels were used. True, most of the paintings (all of them of a devotional nature) were small. By the end of the 15th century, however, panels of considerable size were used. In all, tradition and the generally moderate size of the pictures dictated the choice of wooden panels. In Italy, these panels were made of poplar, pine, etc.; in the North, oak was the material preferred.

The preparation of the surface of these panels, a method dating from antiquity to the 20th century, was identical. First, the panels were sized with a solution of glue water. Next, priming with gesso followed; finally, if oil colors (not tempera) were used, another sizing followed. The task of this last sizing was to isolate the gesso and thus make it largely nonabsorbent for oil painting. The gesso (Italian word for gypsum) was prepared from various white pigments (chalk, gypsum, etc.) bound by size.

Now, I shall not recommend the use of classic gessoing because, under today's conditions, it has become entirely obsolete. Today, preparation of panels is very simple. In the first place, untempered Masonite boards, $1/8''$ thick, are preferable to any other material, because of Masonite's great toughness and resistance to changes in atmospheric moisture. Liquitex Gesso, or a similar acrylic emulsion, should be used, thinned with water to the consistency of milk. *This thin consistency prevents the forming of brush marks,* which result in undesirable textural effects when they appear on a panel's priming. Brush the thinned emulsion to the *smooth* side of the support; after one coat has dried, a second application should be made. That is all there is to it. No sandpapering is required, nor any other treatment except for the imprimatura (a preliminary wash of color).

### ADVANTAGES AND DISADVANTAGES OF PANELS

Why and when should one choose a panel? In the first place, consider the size of the painting. For anything smaller than $12'' \times 16''$, a panel is preferable because small paintings call for extra smooth surfaces, even if the subject does not require a miniaturistic or detailed approach.

As I have stated previously, knife work cannot be successful on a rigid surface; however, if done on a small area, the difficulty can be overcome.

In general, smoothness of the support is a disadvantage in *large* sizes, for a painting may easily become tenuous. Impasti do not look attractive when painted on panels. Of course, I am thinking here of contemporary painting (other than nonobjective); the large wooden panels of the old masters (used well into the 17th century) are ruled by a different esthetic.

But there are other considerations when working on a panel, such as the problems of *underpainting*. As I have mentioned, a knife does not work well on the toothless surface of a panel. Instead, use a bristle brush for underpainting; then smooth its harsh demarcations with a soft hair blender. However, a panel is ideal for alla prima painting, as discussed in Chapter 9.

Masonite panels (larger than 20″ x 24″) are apt to warp. Hence they will require supporting crossbars or frames, glued to the inside surface. A panel ¼″ thick will not have a tendency to warp, but it will be quite heavy. To avoid warping, it is advisable not to *drench* a panel with the gesso solution, but to use a brush dipped in it lightly.

When, for some reason, you are thinking of painting on a wooden support, the acrylic priming material is best. The same priming material is also best for supports such as gypsum or cement walls.

### MISCELLANEOUS MATERIALS

Before discussing colors and their diluents (the choice of which is of paramount importance in painting), let us review some useful minor paraphernalia.

*Charcoal:* Before beginning a painting, you will make a preliminary sketch, or an exact drawing, depending on your method of working. The best material for this purpose is *vine charcoal,* sold in sticks. A pencil or charcoal pencil is not satisfactory because its marks cannot be removed easily. Charcoal pencil, especially, leaves strong black marks, which can become quite a problem to erase. Vine charcoal, on the other hand, can be easily wiped off with a kneaded eraser or a piece of chamois or cheesecloth, which can be used indefinitely for this purpose. When more complex compositions are planned, your drawing should be done first on paper.

*Tracing paper* is best for this purpose because it can be wiped clean of charcoal marks more easily than any other paper. Furthermore, this sleek paper is best suited for tracing a drawing onto the canvas. For transferring a drawing to the canvas use *graphite paper; carbon paper should never be used* as its marks will bleed through any layer of paint put on top of it. *Transfer paper* can be easily prepared in the studio. Simply cover a piece of tracing paper with charcoal or graphite dust or, still better, use a dry pigment such as Venetian red or umber. These colors can be rubbed in with a piece of cloth. The paper will serve for any number of tracings. For strong tracings on large surfaces, it is practical to mix one of these dry pigments with kerosene or turpentine. Then, brush it on an absorbent paper such as newsprint. (The brushed-on pigment will not adhere to the slick surface of the tracing paper.)

The way to make the tracing on the canvas indelible is simply to spray it with *fixative*.

Thus far, your list of equipment necessary for painting includes: brushes in both categories, bristle and sable; painting knives; canvas and stretchers; panels; charcoal; tracing paper; transfer paper; and fixative. Next comes the list of colors, and then, the painting media.

# CHAPTER 3
# *Colors*

Do you require a special range of colors for landscape painting? There is little doubt about it because the variety of objects in landscapes can be very extensive. Of course, it could be maintained that a masterpiece of landscape painting could be done with four colors, or perhaps less. In art history, such examples exist in profusion. However, one painter may prefer a wide range of colors; another painter may prefer a different range. Therefore, in this chapter, I shall try to satisfy the most ravenous appetites for colors, and list all the useful and permanent ones.

### COMPLETE LIST OF COLORS

First, the ones possessing the lowest chroma: white and black. The former should be *flake white;* we might just as well forget about any other kind of white. We have two distinctly different *blacks:* ivory and Mars black. *Blues:* you will need three: Prussian, ultramarine, and phthalo blue. *Greens:* viridian, phthalo green, and chrome oxide green dull. All these are referred to as *cold* colors.

Warm colors start with the *yellows:* Naples yellow, yellow ochre, dark ochre, Mars yellow, raw siena, strontium yellow, zinc yellow, cadmium yellow (light, dark, and cadmium orange), and Hansa yellow. Eleven of these may seem to make a long list; but experience teaches us that at one time or another one of these will be a welcome "find."

Of the *reds* we have: cadmium red light, Venetian red, Mars violet, and the purplish alizarin crimson; four in all. There are four *browns:* burnt siena, burnt and raw umber, Mars brown.

These add up to twenty-eight colors, a formidable number. But I repeat: although at times only one fourth of the range may go into action, you can derive much pleasure and inspiration from experimenting with this or that "exotic" color. If we speak of the exotic, in fact, only the Mars colors are not yet considered part of the standard list. While my choice of yellows appears to be very large, all those listed are primary colors; that is, none can be obtained by intermixture with other colors. When working with colors, you should always keep in mind that it is best to obtain the largest variety of effects from the narrowest choice of colors. That is, through experience, you should develop the faculty of intermixing as few colors as possible, rather than calling for the "tactical" support of an additional color.

Here are the general principles of mixing colors: (1) For any desired effect, use only three different colors (in addition to white, if required). The reason for this is simple: it would be difficult, if not impossible, to remember and later duplicate a larger color combination. (2) Only colors of compatible strength should be intermixed. It would be useless to mix a strong with a weak color; the first would nullify the effects of the second. (3) Differentiate between the colors used for underpainting and overpainting. (Briefly: underpainting colors should be *body colors*, that is, poor in oil content; overpainting colors should be richer in oil.) Concluding, I should say that all colors listed here are permanent, as well as chemically compatible.

### FLAKE WHITE

It is an obvious fact that modern chemistry has provided the painter with a large range of superior colors. Science has not, however, created a white for artist's use that can equal the white lead (the modern tube color is called flake white) which has been used for thousands of years. There are modern whites infinitely superior to the old standbys, but these are useful only for industrial purposes, and only where oil is *not* the binder for the pigment. Hence, we might as well forget about the widely advertised —and widely used—titanium and zinc whites. As I have mentioned in some of my other books, these whites should be rejected by the judicious painter.

Suffice it to say that *flake white* is the densest of all the colors on the palette; it enters every picture in far greater quantity than any other color, for nearly all colors become intermixed with it. Flake white in tubes dries moderately well and has good covering capacity. Its opacity, however, is far below that of titanium white.

### IVORY BLACK AND MARS BLACK

Ivory and Mars blacks are two distinctly different colors used, as a rule, for different purposes. In comparison with ivory black, the chief characteristics of Mars black are: greater density (hence greater opacity); stronger tinting capacity (that is, imparting its own color to others); and a much faster rate of drying.

These characteristics, however, do not make ivory black less useful. On the contrary, one could consider ivory black indispensable, whereas the use of Mars black calls for a certain sophistication in painting technique. The color value of ivory black is deeper, more luminous and velvety, and its moderate strength is easier to control in mixtures. Mars black, because of its great strength, is something for the connoisseur to contend with. These characteristics point to specific uses for these colors. Ivory black is desirable for every occasion except where you want to produce an impasto. Mars black is suitable for impasti, and for the most forceful applications of pure or nearly pure black color.

Now, you might ask why so much fuss is made over black for the purpose of landscape painting. But you should remember that *black is very important for producing greens,* and for dulling other colors or color combinations that may appear to be too high in key.

### PRUSSIAN BLUE

Prussian blue, because of its versatility, is the most important blue on our palette. Next to phthalo blue, it has the greatest tinting power. However, it differs from other blues in several respects: it has a greenish cast, giving green nuances in intermixtures more easily, and it dries more quickly. Because of its powerful hue and transparency, Prussian blue cannot be used in its pure form—in broad applications—without intermixture with another color. It may, of course, be used pure in delineations.

### PHTHALO BLUE

Phthalo blue is just as strong and even more transparent than Prussian blue, but it dries slowly. What most concerns us is that its tonal value is completely different from Prussian blue. The best way to arrive at a comparison of tonal values is to mix the color with white. Sometimes such mixtures show dramatic differences. The difference between these two blues is the clear, "celestial" blue of the phthalo; I call it thus, because it reminds me of the clear blue color of the ancient lapis lazuli found in medieval paintings and illuminated manuscripts.

But there is one disadvantage when you wish to mix phthalo blue with warm colors such as umber. Whereas umber and Prussian blue (with white) will give us an endless and most beautiful variety of grays, the grays produced with phthalo blue and umber have a narrower range and a purplish cast.

### ULTRAMARINE BLUE

Ultramarine has a distinctly purplish cast when mixed with white. This blue became popular when Impressionist painters clamored for purples which worked well with yellows and orange to produce sunlit effects. Neutral ultramarine (without a purple cast) is not available in tubes, but it can be obtained in pigment form. However, this neutral hue differs little from the one that can be produced with phthalo blue. In all, ultramarine has a much weaker tinting capacity; for landscape painting, however, I consider it indispensable.

### VIRIDIAN GREEN

Viridian green is (like blue, yellow, and red) a primary color—one that cannot be obtained through intermixtures of other colors. Its transparency, drying capacity, and tinting strength are like those of ultramarine—moderate in all these respects.

### PHTHALO GREEN

This green is related in color to viridian, but its tinting capacity is vastly superior, its transparency considerably greater, and its drying time longer. Because of its intense tinting strength, this color should be used chiefly for emergencies —when you require a radical, quick change in an existing color combination. Thus, we can consider this green a powerful "persuader."

### CHROME OXIDE GREEN DULL

A green of considerable covering capacity; chrome oxide is totally opaque, very dense, and has great tinting strength. It may not be used habitually in landscapes, but when the need arises, it is good to have a tube ready. Interestingly, a similar hue can be produced easily by mixing together the colors you clean off the palette after all the work is done, and adding a strong yellow (such as cadmium) to these waste colors.

### NAPLES YELLOW

Why do we deal with Naples yellow first? Because it has a milder hue than any other of our yellows. It is also the least aggressive, and one that cannot be easily associated with a concrete object. Therefore, Naples yellow is best used for *distances* where all the objects are conditioned by atmospheric effects.

Atmospheric effects suggest transparency, inasmuch as the solid matter, seen at a distance, takes on a less substantial appearance. (But this pertains only to retinal and psychological sensations.) However, in oil painting, distant objects will have to be handled with *opaque* colors, since "bleached out" effects require mixtures of white lead, a color of considerable opacity. In fact, Naples (chemically a lead antimoniate) is very much related to white lead.

### YELLOW OCHRE

This color, often called *light ochre*, is also a nonaggressive yellow of the brown variety, suggesting organic matter. We can associate it easily with substances such as wood, vegetation, or solid inorganic material, such as sand and stone. Hence, its effects are warmer and more substantial than those of Naples yellow. Ochre is opaque and dries moderately well. It is one of the most important earth colors ( chiefly a composition of clay and iron oxide found in natural deposits).

## BROWN OCHRE

As its name indicates, this is a dark variety of ochre—a color for lazy people, if I may say so, because mixtures of yellow ochre and umber will duplicate its tint. However, when one is driven by a momentary "creative impulse," it is useful to have such a color ready because it can then easily be conditioned by the addition of another color.

## MARS YELLOW

This yellow is an artificial ochre (iron oxide), and you should use it when you require an ochre of greater tinting capacity. It is more transparent than ochre, and dries, like all the Mars colors, considerably faster. The nuances produced by mixing Mars yellow with the cold colors are different from ochre mixtures. Hence Mars yellow is helpful occasionally whenever you tire of the often prosaic yellow ochre mixtures.

## RAW SIENA

Raw siena is a yellow-brown, transparent color. You may ask why I suggest so many of the rather closely related earth colors for your palette. The answer is simple: the drabness of the yellow-brown range is alleviated if, from time to time, variations of similar colors are called into action.

## STRONTIUM AND ZINC YELLOWS

These are "esoteric" colors, inasmuch as they are seldom used by the uninitiated. In instances when the "brassy" cadmium yellow appears too active and there is no way to put a damper on it effectively (an addition of white would merely make it brighter), what kind of yellow would do better than strontium? Moreover, in mixtures with other colors, strontium yellow offers a number of entirely different shades than those obtained from cadmium yellow mixtures.

As for zinc yellow, it has greater usefulness in still life painting, but I would not neglect to place it on my palette when special coloristic effects are desired. Mixtures with these yellows (particularly those with blues) have their own intrinsic beauty.

## CADMIUM YELLOW LIGHT, DARK, AND CADMIUM ORANGE

Since their high chroma brings every object into the forefront, this group belongs to the class of aggressive, "brassy" yellows. These are the *local* colors—the colors of objects seen close at hand—as opposed to atmospheric colors found in the distance. But this is not an accusation—far from it, for without the cadmiums there would be no life for the landscape painter! These colors are so important that only the best quality should be considered. Therefore, avoid cheap, bargain-price cadmiums.

I mentioned cadmium yellow light and dark because the *dark* is quite indispensable in certain situations; there is no way of darkening a cadmium through some admixture. However, cadmium orange is assuredly for the lazy; it can be produced easily by mixing cadmium yellow (light or dark) with cadmium red. All best quality cadmiums have excellent tinting capacity, but they are slow driers.

## HANSA YELLOW

This is prepared from an aniline dye. It is absolutely permanent and most useful in glazing and in mixtures with flake white for underpainting.

## CADMIUM RED LIGHT

I refer to cadmium red light *only* (not to the darker varieties) because you can obtain any degree of darkness by smaller or larger admixtures of alizarin crimson. Moreover, it is only on the rarest occasion that a landscape painter would find use for a flamboyant color. For the landscape painter, cadmium red light is the most brilliant color of them all; it is the equivalent of the color known as vermilion. What sensations of color does the very word *vermilion* bring before our inner eye! But, rhapsodizing aside, it is a happy painter who finds an occasion to use this brilliant hue.

## ALIZARIN CRIMSON

This is the most transparent and the slowest dryer of all the reds. It is also the most problematic color in landscape painting.

In flamboyant sunsets, it will do just what is expected of it, provided the painter handles such "dangerous" subject matter with discretion! For we all know how quickly flamboyance can turn a picture into a "chromo" or a "calendar picture." In works of this kind, how often we see the amateur blissfully mixing alizarin crimson, ultramarine, and white for those beloved purple mountains in the far distance. Indeed, although in nature no color is intrinsically "bad," in a painting some colors do set our teeth on edge.

However, I mention this color in connection with landscape painting because someone might be able to manage it properly, even though most painters cannot.

## VENETIAN RED

This red, on the other hand, is a pedestrian, prosaic color; but, like bread and butter, it is a necessity. An earth color, it is among the most powerful on our palette. Other varieties—often designated as light red, terra rosa, or terra di Pozzuoli—possess much weaker tints; but, by the same token, they are just as valuable. All these iron oxides are opaque and moderately well drying.

## MARS VIOLET

Mars violet's tinting capacity and opacity match any of the strongest colors on this list. Its rich, dark tone has great solemnity and resonance.

## BURNT SIENA

This is a rather commonplace red-brown color when used undiluted; thinned with the medium, however, a beautiful glowing color results, ideal for glazing. It is the second fastest drying color on our palette.

## UMBER, BURNT AND RAW

Umbers are the best driers. The difference between the kinds called *burnt* and *raw* is slight in most brands. Burnt umber has a warm cast; raw umber, to be of value, has to be dark grayish-brown. Unfortunately, this is not always the case with every make. Although these are drab, unexciting colors, they are important not only for various color mixtures, but also as additives, to accelerate the drying of all other colors.

## MARS BROWN

This color rarely appears on the painter's palette. Superficially, it resembles umber, but its tone is much deeper, its opacity and tinting strength greater, and it can be very effective when judiciously used. It is an excellent dryer, like all the Mars colors. However, when mixed with white, its coloristic effects are certainly not among the happiest.

## PRINCIPAL CHARACTERISTICS OF COLORS

The color characteristics that concern us most are: tinting strength, transparency or opacity, and drying properties.

Transparency indicates that the pigments were compounded with a considerable amount of the vehicle (usually linseed oil); these are known as glazing colors. *Glazing* means covering a light surface with a transparent *darker color*. Opaque colors are called body colors.

Try to familiarize yourself with comparative drying properties. The quickest drying colors are: umber, burnt siena, Prussian blue, and most of the Mars colors. The slowest are ivory black, alizarin crimson, phthalo colors, and cadmiums. However, because of measures taken by some manufacturers, colors may behave differently than indicated here. Any slow drying color can be made to change its native characteristics by intermixture with faster drying colors or with faster drying painting media, discussed in the next chapter.

# CHAPTER 4
# *Paint diluents*

All pigments are dispersed in a vehicle, thus forming paint. In the consistency that comes from the tube, paint is rarely used without a diluent called "painting medium," which has one foremost task: to improve the working qualities of the paint material.

The conscientious manufacturer does the best he can for his products under present-day conditions. Are these conditions ideal? Compared to those that prevailed a century or even half a century ago, they certainly are. Yet tube paint is quite deficient in the quality of its body.

### SHORT PAINT VS. LONG

If the body of paint is *short,* it lacks viscosity. Such paint, when heaped on the palette or moved with the brush, retains its configuration (Fig. 14). In contrast, *long* paint is viscous; depending on the degree of viscosity, it will form soft configurations. In other words, long paint will seek its level. In extreme form, we know this condition from the behavior of enamel paints.

Why is tube paint short, and why is this undesirable? We can observe that the old masters' paints were always long. Now, let us look at our modern tube paint more closely.

We may assume that it is compounded with the proper quantity of pigment and with the best available vehicle—linseed oil. Of course, modern paint is more finely ground than the ancient pigment because grinding is now done by mechanical means. However—and this is the crucial point—modern paint is hermetically encased in a metal tube, thus preventing the oil from becoming *polymerized. Polymerization (a form of molecular change in the oil) accounts for the viscosity of the paint body.*

Moreover, to remain in brushable condition —that is, to prevent pigment and oil separation and consequent hardening of paint—the manufacturer has to condition the paint with a material known as *aluminum stearate,* a metallic soap. It is an accepted norm that a 2% addition does not impair the quality of the product, but the aluminum stearate certainly is responsible for its shortness.

Figure 14A  Textures produced with the brush, and stippled effects made with a painting knife, using paint as it comes from the tube. Paint referred to as *short* forms hard, crisp configurations.

## FUNCTION OF PAINTING MEDIA

An important rule to remember: in the classic technique with which this book is concerned, never use short paint as it comes from the tube without improving it by adding conditioners and paint diluents discussed later in this chapter.

The painting diluents to which I refer (under the discussion of Copal Painting Media) make the paint more responsive to the action of the brush. The conditioner (Copal Concentrate), which radically changes the body of paint, is a separate product. To repeat, a painting medium *dilutes* the tube color.

Which medium is the most appropriate for this purpose? Assuredly, the one that most closely approximates the qualities found in the media of the most accomplished technicians in art history—the early Flemish masters.

To best serve our purposes, a medium should: (1) impart a certain viscosity to the paint; (2) increase the paint's adhesive properties; (3) safeguard the permanence of a painting.

To elaborate further on these three points, what is the effect of paint viscosity? It promotes the fusion of paints; that is, it facilitates their blending. Because of the increased resilience in the paint body, you can superimpose paints while painting wet-in-wet.

How can you increase the paints' adhesive power? Here it must be understood that linseed oil alone—under favorable circumstances—can fulfill this task adequately. Linseed oil in combination with a resin can do it much better, as well as allow certain manipulations of paint which absolutely require the addition of resin. When you apply paints very thinly for glazing, only the presence of resin makes it possible for the paint material to adhere to the vertically placed support, and not drip off the surface.

Lastly, we expressed our concern for permanence. Does linseed oil fail in this respect? Not at all; if used sparingly, it has all the properties necessary for permanence. However, even the best grades of linseed oil are subject to yellowing. And, if you use the thermally processed form of linseed oil known as *stand oil,* the viscosity of paint will materially improve. (Stand oil is produced by cooking linseed oil in the

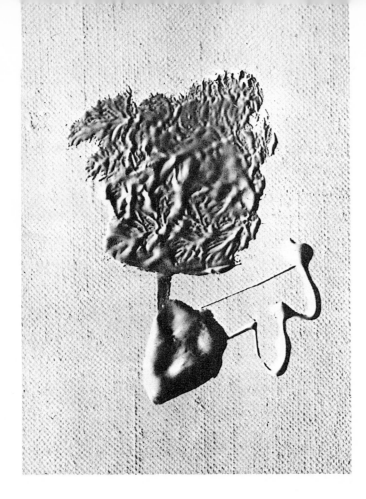

Figure 14B  Paint conditioned by Copal Concentrate forms soft, rounded textures. It is called *long*.

absence of oxygen; this process, to a large extent, prevents the oil from yellowing.)

## SOFT AND HARD RESINS

Before discussing the problem of permanence—a problem which involves resins—let me briefly describe the nature of these substances. The resins with which we are concerned are exudates of certain coniferous trees, and can be divided into two general groups: soft and hard resins.

Soft resins are produced by living trees; hard resins are exudates of fossilized trees, now extinct. A medium containing a soft resin will impair the permanence of a painting because paint mixed with it remains forever soluble, even under the mildest solvents. *Soft resins should be used only for varnishing;* those commonly used for this purpose are *damar* and *mastic.*

Hard resins, on the other hand, polymerize with age, reduce the porosity of the linoxyn (dried paint film), and thus prevent the incorporation of dirt into the paint film. Scientific research has proven that the stability of this film is improved in the presence of the resin. The only hard resin with which the painter is concerned is Congo copal.

## COPAL PAINTING MEDIA

Some obsolete texts assert that copal resin "causes darkening and embrittlement of the paint film." This misunderstanding was caused by the fact that one of the famous earlier technicians, Max Doerner (who was also my teacher in Munich, almost a half century ago), used a copal preparation which was produced from an inferior open-kettle boiled oil, copal, and an addition of 10% of manganese dryer (50 times more than the allowable minimum). This concoction of English origin was well adapted for painting coaches, outdoor signs, etc., but was wholly unsuited for fine art painting.

When I recognized the insufficiency of the damar painting medium (whose faults were later confirmed by the world's foremost authorities), I found that the working qualities of ex-

**Figure 15A** *Landscape with Apollo and Daphne* (16″ x 20″). On the detail (15B), the effects of long paint are clearly discernible in the background, where they form a striated pattern; these strokes were made with the scriptliner. In the second detail (15C), long paint is seen in the light delineations. The sketchy appearance of the foliage shows the marks of a large round sable brush, held sideways.

15B

15C

**Figure 16** *The Old Tree*
(10″ x 12″). On this small, fine-textured canvas, extra long paint was used for the light, calligraphic strokes which show considerable impasto. All details were executed with the scriptliner; the sky and the ground with the painting knife.

isting copal formulations did not meet my demands. Therefore, I set out to perfect the formula and to approximate it as closely as possible to that used by the early Flemish technical wizards. These experiments resulted in Copal Painting Medium Light and Heavy, Copal Concentrate, and Copal Varnish, all introduced by Permanent Pigments of Cincinnati, Ohio, twenty-five years ago. Today, they are widely used in many countries.

Copal Painting Medium Light differs from the heavy quality only in viscosity. That is, the stand oil in the medium possesses a higher degree of polymerization. Actually, personal preference should decide the choice of one medium or the other.

Copal Concentrate is a very special ingredient; its introduction was suggested to me from the description of the material (and its preparation) contained in the well known ancient manuscript of the monk, Theophilus Presbyter. To use it with paint, do the following: with a painting knife, scoop a drop of concentrate, the size of a pea, and mix well with about ½″ of paint as it comes from the tube. Thus, before you start to paint, add the concentrate to every single color—but twice as much to flake white. This is *necessary* because white lead stiffens (due to the rapid formation of lead soap in the compound of lead carbonate) when only a little of the concentrate is added to it.

All colors conditioned by the concentrate become more supple and flowing; their capacity to blend greatly increases; and their depth of color is enhanced. (In Fig. 16, *The Old Tree*, 10″ x 12″, note how the long paint applied with the scriptliner marks the picture with incisive delineations.) When too much of the concentrate is added, the paint becomes enamel-like. This should be taken into consideration when you use the material.

All the copal media promote better drying of paint, improve the quality of the linoxyn (the dried linseed oil film) and, quite important, allow frequent overpainting of surfaces that have not completely solidified. Yellowing and darkening, even in the thinnest applications (those possessing an abundance of the thinner), are obviated; cracking of the paint film *due to internal causes*—that is, chemical changes—will never occur. Here one must distinguish between these chemical changes and damage done by *external* causes, such as pressure against an aged layer of thick paint.

## OTHER DILUENTS AND LIQUIDS

Finally, some comments on other liquids used by the painter. *Cobalt drier* is by far the best of all the existing preparations which accelerate drying of paint. But even this drier must be used sparingly: one drop to about 1″ of the paint as it comes from the tube; one drop to about two teaspoonfuls of the medium. Only thin applications of paint should be conditioned by the drier, since a skin forms quickly on top of the paint layer and prevents the paint within from drying. *If used excessively, even the best quality dryer will cause the paint film to yellow and become brittle.*

Lastly, I must mention the medium still popular among the uninformed, the one I consider quite inferior: linseed oil thinned with turpentine. Moreover, beware of using turpentine alone as a paint thinner, for this liquid destroys the binding property of the oil. However, turpentine is useful in preventing trickling of paint, and, of course, it will soften semisolid paint and well-hardened varnish films. (For trickling, see Chapter 9.)

This ends the list and description of all the materials and their properties which the painter requires. Now we shall proceed to the business of painting landscapes of every conceivable kind.

# CHAPTER 5

# *Pictorial composition*

We all are faced continuously with the issues of composition, not only in art, but in our daily encounters with visual matters. Composition is concerned with the placement and interrelation of objects in space—the manner in which we arrange furniture in a room, fruit in a bowl, or flowers in a vase. The position our body takes (that is, the placement of limbs), the arrangement of rock masses in the Grand Canyon, the constellations of celestial bodies—all form compositions.

Because we constantly face problems of composition, perhaps our awareness of harmony or disharmony becomes more acute. We could say that most of us have an innate feeling for balance and harmony because, even without specialized training, we are able to appraise harmonious proportions and see the balanced position of objects in a given space. For example, even an untrained eye can often determine whether one shape of a window is better proportioned than another, or placed more harmoniously on a facade. Again, practically everyone can see whether or not a piece of fur-

niture is placed in proper relation to other objects in a room; thus, when moving a chair, for example, from one position to another, the arranger calls upon his instinctive sense to create a balanced composition.

## PROBLEMS OF COMPOSITION

What are the problems of composition in the art of painting? They do not differ from the problems we face when we perceive any visual matter on an esthetic level. But in composition, we consider the formal relations that are at the core of every pictorial organization. ("Formal relations" means the interaction between generalized, more or less geometric forms, not specific forms like the shape of a teapot or a maple tree.)

Now, when we speak of *beauty* in a painting, it is not necessarily the same as, or even related to, beauty found in nature. As a matter of fact, things that we may find beautiful in nature (such as a brilliant sunset or a picturesque ruin) may not make a "beautiful picture" unless

**Figure 17** Symmetrical arrangements of objects rob the eye of the incentive for exploration; the mind at once precalculates the strategy of the composition.

translated into suitable pictorial equivalents.

However, the laws of composition—the laws of balance, order, and harmony—are constant. They are independent of any other considerations which act upon our esthetic sensibilities. Thus, differences in the manner of composing a picture due to different styles of painting do not influence the basic laws—mathematical laws, I am tempted to say—of composition. Regardless of how much one style may *seem* to differ from another, all compositions are ruled by the same principles of balance and order which are responsible for the sensation of harmony.

This all points to the importance of a good composition in picture making, for a faulty composition will invalidate all the good qualities a painting may possess.

Today, the words *composition* and *design* are commonly used interchangeably. However, a semantic distinction should be made between them. The word, *design,* if we consider it etymologically, refers to a two-dimensional arrangement of lines; therefore, its character is *plani-*

*metric. Composition,* on the other hand, indicates the presence of a third dimension, which in painting (or drawing) gives the illusion of depth. When considering depth, we shall have to deal with perspective. (Problems of perspective will be discussed later in this chapter.)

### NATURE OF COMPOSITION

I referred to *balance* and *order* which a composition may or may not possess. Let us see what obligations these impose on us. Balance is so easily achieved in pictorial composition that it hardly has special merit. Balance simply means that objects are placed in such relationships that the picture neither falls apart nor tips to one side or another. Balance can be achieved by obvious and commonplace means. But it requires inventiveness to imbue a composition with special interest through the use of ingenious devices and unexpected relationships.

For example, symmetry, the state of perfect balance, appears frequently in nature, and comes to mind when we speak of balance. Al-

though symmetry sometimes has a definite function in pictorial composition, it can become tedious when used for the over-all disposition of objects (Fig. 17). Because in pictorial composition a sequence of regularly placed forms is tedious, a picture with symmetrical arrangements can neutralize the beholder's interest. His attention dulled by monotonous repetitions, the beholder finds his imagination stultified; his mind has anticipated the strategy of the composition. This does not mean that a symmetrical division of space by a centrally placed object is wrong; such symmetry can be counteracted by subsidiary *asymmetrical* arrangements (Figs. 18A and 19A).

To digress for a moment, taboos on the use of symmetrical arrangements have been so forcibly impressed upon the student's mind that when he paints a flower still life, for example, he will invariably *avoid* placing the vase in the middle of the canvas. The inexperienced student does not realize that the natural asymmetry of a flower arrangement *requires* the choice of a central position for the static object, the vase.

◀ **Figure 18A** *Spring* (22″ x 44″). The central object, placed directly in the middle, divides the surface into two equal parts—a disadvantageous division; but the great expanse of land in the background shows sufficient variations to intrigue the eye.

◀ **Figure 18B** (detail). The burst of sprouting twigs at the top counteracts the static rise of the tree trunk.

**Figure 19A** *The Edge of the Forest* (20″ x 40″). In this painting, a composition similar to Fig. 18 was used. Here the tree is set against a forest background, and the static position of the tree trunk is opposed by the diagonal thrust of the dead, thin trunk in front of it. The unwavering line of this trunk was painted with the edge of the knife held vertically to the canvas. ▶

**Figure 19B** Detail of branches. ▼

19A

19B

**Figure 20** *River Bend* (16″ x 24″).
This composition did not come
off successfully. The small forms
in the middle and background,
although they show some
variations, are too much alike in
mass. Neither their total mass
nor the area of the foreground
gains dominance; both vie for the
beholder's attention without
quite reaching their aim.

**Figure 21** *The River* (26″ x 36″).
In this picture, the problem has
been solved more adequately.
Here, in spite of the close
relationship of the masses, interest
is kept alive by the rushing flow
of the stream that divides them
—in fact keeps them moving. In
this painting, as well as in most
of my landscapes, the horizon
line is placed high on the picture
plane. This allows the arrangement
of the scenery in a cartographic
manner; thus vast vistas of the
ground can be encompassed. ▶

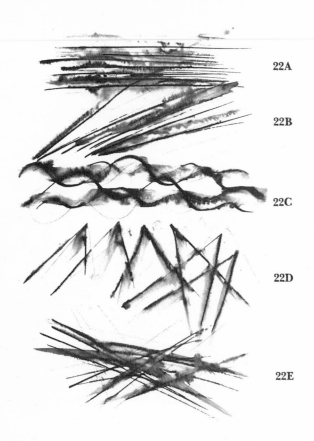

22A

22B

22C

22D

22E

Figure 22A  Parallel lines suggest calm. 22B Diagonal lines imply movement. 22C Undulating lines suggest rhythmic motion. 22D Pyramidal lines with sharp angles create an upward surge. 22E Crisscrossing lines show disorder or animation.

I have given *order* as the second element in pictorial composition; it concerns the harmonious arrangement of diversified forms. While contrast of forms offers interest to the eye, this contrast and diversity should create harmony, rather than confusion. Excessive *uniformity* of form, on the other hand, tends to create monotony (Figs. 20 and 21). In other words, order arises from the presence of harmoniously balanced form relationships; these always induce a pleasurable sensation.

## STRATEGY OF COMPOSITION

As discussed above, the interrelationships of forms in a composition are essentially geometric; we think of them as abstract because they have no associational values, no emotional content. These geometric forms are also relatively static. However, certain directional lines, along which the forms are developed, can have associational values. For example, in Fig. 22, horizontal parallel (or near parallel) lines suggest calm; diagonals—dynamic movement; swerving

motion—rhythm; pyramidal, sharp angles—upward surge; criss-crossing lines—extreme animation.

In the arrangement of landscape motifs, the underlying directional lines tend to form the picture's skeletal framework. Such effects appear in many paintings introduced in this book. For example: the menacing rock formation, in Fig. 23A, becomes strangely pacified by the parallel arrangement of lines at the top. In Fig. 25, the upward movement is suggested by the rising lines. In Fig. 67A, disorder is created by the criss-cross pattern of the fallen logs, and so forth.

## COHERENCE, UNITY, EMPHASIS

Thus far, we have been dealing with formal, or as I have said, *abstract* elements of a composition—those that underlie all subject matter. Once you have determined the theme of a painting, different considerations will arise, namely, how to attract the viewer's attention and then, how to hold it. How can this be

Figure 23A *Mountain Landscape* (40" x 50"). The accent is on the distant mountain panorama; all the subsidiary elements of the composition—the massive rock in the middle (detail 23B), the winding river, and the lack of details in the foreground—direct the beholder's attention to this ultimate climax.

Figure 23B  Detail of rock formation.

done? The answer is: by creating coherence, unity, and emphasis.

*Coherence* is achieved by organizing objects, or groups of objects, so that they relate to one another without forming independent units within the composition.

*Unity* refers to the integration of the picture's motifs to make a homogeneous composition which contains logical associations. For example: a cow would look *right* in a pasture or on a wooden bridge over a creek; but it would be out of place on a steel suspension bridge or on a cement sidewalk. In other words, subject matter must conform to its natural environment; in a surrealistic composition, however, disassociations are striven for.

*Emphasis* is needed to bring a composition to a dramatic climax. Emphasis depends upon the most eloquent presentation of the dominant theme in the composition; all other parts should be subordinated to this dominant motif and

they should not challenge or fight its position (Fig. 23). These subsidiary motifs should not distract the eye or become autonomous, but rather, like road signs, lead the attention to the main theme (Fig. 24). The main theme, however, need not necessarily be represented by one single object. A group of objects can share the dominant area of the composition and unite to function as a climax, as shown in Fig. 25.

To repeat: the task of a composition is to hold the eye within the boundaries of a painting, and to lead the attention of the beholder from one object to another until the work as a whole is taken in. In a well conceived painting, its construction gratifies our curiosity, and also pleases our esthetic sensibilities.

## CHARACTERISTICS OF COMPOSITIONS

When we examine landscape motifs, we become aware of another aspect of pictorial composition: namely, the relationship between dominant objects and the space around them. This

**Figure 26** *After Sunset* (28"x44"). Here one single motif dominates the scene. All other objects appear as subsidiary elements. In this composition, it is the dramatic incident that arrests our attention.

Figure 27 *Western Landscape* (24" x 40"). A group of motifs assume the important role in the composition. The effectiveness of one element is activated by the presence of another element. Here, we can speak of an ensemble where all the instruments together play a chord in a musical composition, without particular emphasis on one or another subject.

Figure 28A  *The Lake* (16″ x 20″). The overall pattern seen in this picture depends on the character of the handwriting—that is, on the calligraphic effect of the linear pattern. These lines were made with round sable brushes and the scriptliner (detail 28B). Only the area of the lake was treated with the painting knife.

Figure 28B  Detail of brushstrokes. ▶

space need not be empty (like a sky, for instance), but can be made up of objects that form the background for the central motif. In the accepted terminology, dominant objects are called *positive,* and background objects, *negative* space.

The interaction of these shapes plays an important role in the structure of a composition. Although the negative shapes do not have decisive weight, or, more accurately, they *should not* have such weight, they can exert a marked influence on the general appearance of a painting. These negative shapes can make the ensemble appear either flimsy or solid; they can add to or detract from the effectiveness of the dominant objects. The *interdependence* of positive and negative shapes is exemplified in Figs. 26 and 27.

In Fig. 28A, in contrast to the preceding example, we may speak of an over-all pattern. It is not easy to decide which system of pictorial organization is the more effective. However, we can say that it is *more difficult* to make an over-all design which sustains the beholder's interest.

In the example in Fig. 29, an ineffectual and disturbing placement of the main motif is seen. This misplacement illustrates the following compositional strategy: if activity centers around the picture's edges, the eye is not invited to explore the central contents of a painting. Physiologically, this occurs because our field of vision is spheroid; the center of our optical lens, the eyeball, sees objects in sharp focus, whereas at its edges our visual field is blurred.

I mentioned that objects which are placed near the boundaries of a painting take our gaze out of the picture, instead of leading our eyes to the center of interest. A similar difficulty arises when the entire vertical side and part of the horizontal side are taken up by a solid mass of subject matter, be it trees, rocks, or other landscape elements. The density of such a mass at once arrests our attention at the picture's edge, and suggests a continuation beyond the picture's frame. This is illustrated in Fig. 30A. In Fig. 30B, an opening has been made in the solid mass of trees, thus forcing our attention into, and not away from, the picture's center.

Figure 29  The main objects placed at the picture's outer edges divert our attention from the central areas where the active elements should be gathered.

Figure 30A  If a mass of objects (trees, rocks, etc.) occupies an entire vertical side and part of a horizontal side of the picture, the weight of the mass will draw the viewer's gaze beyond the picture's frame.

Figure 30B  The activity of the solid, positive space was minimized by inserting negative spaces into the area, thus reducing the weightiness of the whole.

31A

31B

◀ Figure 31A When a few objects are assembled in even numbers, their rhythmic sequence appears monotonous. 31B Uneven numbers form a more interesting rhythm.

Figure 32 When an object is placed at a point that divides a surface into roughly three equal parts, the sensation of perfect balance is created. Such a division of a surface is known as the "golden section." ▼

In Fig. 31, situations are demonstrated that cannot easily be explained in words, for they are strictly optical. An even number of objects assembled on the picture's plane does not create an interesting rhythm. An uneven number provides a more effective sequence. Of course, this refers to a *small* number of objects where their rhythmical interaction is quite apparent.

Another optical phenomenon can be found in the so-called *golden section* (Fig. 32). Here, the object is positioned to divide the entire surface into three approximately equal parts. It is difficult to explain why such placement of the main object creates perfect balance, but perhaps a mathematically inclined mind would be satisfied to know that the golden section is "that part of a line, or space, in which the size of the smaller part is to the size of the greater part as the greater part is to the whole." This equation was already known in antiquity.

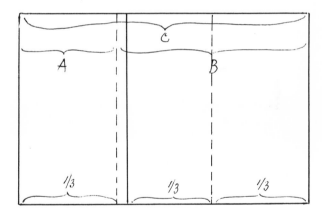

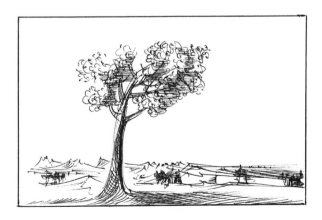

# CHAPTER 6

# *Perspective, picture format, light and shade*

We have referred to two-dimensional design as linear. Hence, it does not suggest spatial recession, or at least there is no emphasis on forms "in the round." A mere landscape *design* can only be conceived as a decorative flat pattern, vertically and horizontally arranged. As an end in itself, a landscape design—an arrangement of flat shapes and lines on a flat surface—is of no interest to us, for our task is to arrange objects in three-dimensional *space,* which can be shallow, or can extend into an indefinite distance.

### FOREGROUND, MIDDLEGROUND, BACKGROUND

When we discuss *shallow* and *indefinite* space, we have to consider the foreground, middleground, and background. A shallow space will, of necessity, be limited to the foreground only. A deeper recession will add a middleground, which can be placed near or far, but not in the ultimate distance (the line of the unobstructed horizon, which is the maximum depth our vision can reach). These arrangements in depths are illustrated in Fig. 33. Examples of paintings showing such spatial arrangements are seen in Figs. 34, 35, and 36.

These illustrations help the landscape painter to realize the meaning of the ancient Chinese landscape painters who observed: "In the distance lies the enchantment of landscape." The secret of the attraction of distances lies in the stirring of our imagination. Whereas nearby objects reveal their "secrets" readily, our imagination becomes galvanized by the veiled "goings on" in the distance. This does not mean that objects placed close to us cannot be conceived imaginatively. But experience shows that the landscape painter deprives himself of an important pictorial instrument when he limits himself to shallow space.

When observing perspective in Fig. 33, two important characteristics emerge. In Fig. 33A, the sensation of recession is brought about by placing a number of objects one in front of another, thus suggesting their different positions in space. In this system, even the largest object or mass can maintain the most distant position. In Fig. 33C, the illusion of depth is created in

**33A**

**33B**

Figure 33  Principal arrangements of objects in space. 33A Placement in foreground only; middleground and background are not in evidence. 33B Foreground and middleground are considered. 33C  The entire spatial recession is brought into sight.

two ways: first, by the progressive diminution of objects as they recede; second, by parallel lines converging at the vanishing point on the horizon. The system in Fig. 33B is considered "modern;" we see it fully adopted and developed in Cézanne's work. Fig. 33C exemplifies the classic system.

### HISTORY OF PERSPECTIVE

When I refer to a "modern" and a "classic" system, I make this distinction merely to clarify, and not to persuade that this or that method is the proper one for dealing with spatial problems. The invention—or rather the full development—of classic or scientific perspective (as it is often called) took place at the beginning of the Renaissance. This conception of perspective (as well as the newly developed science of anatomy), became the guiding principle of Renaissance masters; with them it was a creative pursuit, accounting for some of the greatest achievements of the classic school of painting.

The science of perspective was formulated,

purportedly, by Euclid. Some of its principles were said to have been applied by Polygnotus (5th century B.C.), who used foreshortening in his figures to suggest spatial depth. Later, the achitect Vitruvius (1st century B.C.) refers to empirical (that is, scientific) perspective in his writings, and we find its application in murals from Pompeii.

In medieval times, the problems of geometric perspective were treated by various scholastic writers such as Roger Bacon, Vitellio, and Percham. However, the first systematic and comprehensive description of the rules of perspective was given in Piero della Francesca's book, written between 1470 and 1490, although not printed until 1899. Other treatises on perspective were made by Paolo Uccello, by the architect Leon Battista Alberti, and of course, by Leonardo da Vinci and Dürer.

However, before the Italians, Flemish painters discovered the laws of empirical perspective through mere observation, not by the scientific means employed by the Italians. Great as the discovery was, by the middle of the 16th century

59

◄ Figure 34   *Dark Forest* (12″ x 16″).
A thick, dark growth of trees,
showing a variety of textures,
silhouetted against the light sky.
The trees form the foreground,
and shut off space at the picture
plane. To heighten the eerie mood
of the picture, the sky was painted
in a light pink (Venetian red
and white), tinged here and there
with a trace of viridian green.

▲ Figure 35   *The Inlet* (12″ x 16″).
The sketchily treated foreground
of this small alla prima painting
allows the attention of the
viewer to concentratate on the
middleground. The serpentine
movement of the shoreline, stopped
at the left side by the tree, as
well as the chain of mountains
at the top, help sustain attention
on the painting's central motifs.

Figure 36   *The Isthmus*
(16″ x 22″). The small basin in
front, with the rocks and clumps
of trees pointing straight up,
take the eye along the jagged
shore of the waterway directly
to the furthermost distance. ▶

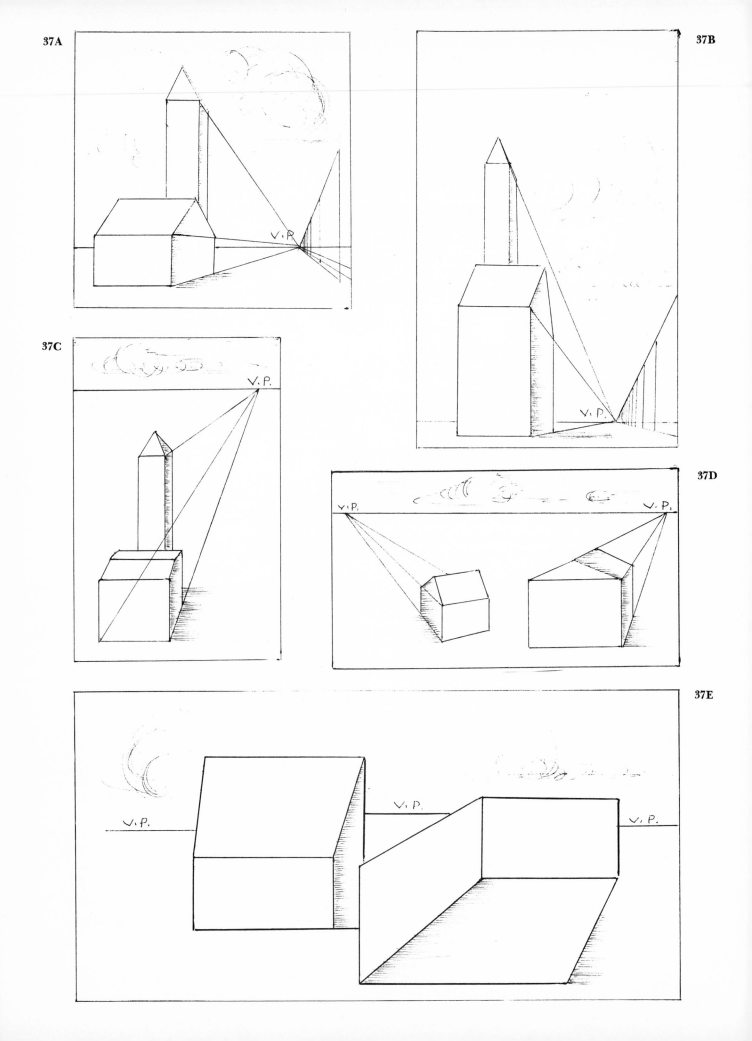

37A

37B

37C

37D

37E

V.P.

**Figure 37A** The viewer and the objects are placed on the same level. **37B** The viewer sees objects as if he were sitting on the ground; such a point of observation is called a "worm's eye view," hence, the low horizon line. **37C** The objects are seen from high above, so the horizon line is high; this type of landscape appears as if it were seen from a "bird's eye view." **37D** Objects are placed in different positions with different vanishing points on the horizon. **37E** Anarchy is the ruling principle, for the same object is seen from more than one vantage point (parallels do not converge as they recede); here the rules of empirical perspective do not apply. We see such a chaos of perspective in medieval paintings, and also in those by Cézanne and many contemporary painters. However, we notice arrangements of this nature only when solid objects are used, and in landscapes where there are dwellings. For example, the roof of a house may be represented as if seen from a high position, and the ground level as if it were viewed from a lower vantage point. Is such an unsystematic use of perspective wrong? Far from it. No artistic system can be considered inviolable; it all depends on the manner of its use.

the system had lost its magic and its significance. By the end of the century (with the Baroque painters), it had become a devitalized scheme without esthetic importance.

Why do I offer all these "facts and figures" about scientific perspective? I hope to impress upon the student that this system is not the *sine qua non* in art. No matter how correctly the plan may be mapped out, it will not help the painter to elevate his artistic stature. Since most doctrines are dictated by ephemeral vagaries of taste, there is no intrinsic merit in "correctly" applied principles of scientific perspective. We may even say that strict adherence to these principles may easily stultify the student's artistic endeavors. In other words, the probity of a composition in contemporary painting does not depend on *correctness,* but rather on the *ingenuity* of the artist's devices in the realm of perspective.

In Fig. 37A-D, scientific perspective is presented in its simplest form. In Fig. 37E, its rules are consciously ignored, as in medieval painting, before the Renaissance discoveries.

## SHARP FOCUS – SOFT FOCUS

We can say that when painting a landscape, we compromise between what we see and what we know; *knowing* is a composite of all kinds of experience, visual as well as mental. For example, we know that a tree seen in the distance has differentiated leaves, although they appear as a solid mass to our eye. In other words, natural phenomena are not depicted with strictly photographic objectivity.

Let us now consider a composition involving motifs in the foreground, middleground, and background. Normally, we are able to visualize the nearest objects more closely than objects in the distance; that is, objects close to you will appear in sharp focus (hard edges) and the distant objects will be more or less blurred (soft edges). I use the qualification, "normally," because a sharp or blurred focus depends on several considerations: the condition of the atmosphere (dry or moist air), the physiology of our eye, and the style of our painting.

Actually, it is the *style,* rather than the optical considerations, which determines whether you use hard or soft edges in your painting. (Some examples of styles that have influenced the painter's approach are discussed in the final chapter.)

Oil paint can be handled to produce hard or soft edges (also called *contours*), that is, hard or soft divisions between the objects. The preference for one method or another depends on the personal taste of the painter. Since all methods are subject to temporary fashions, any dogmatic acceptance of this or that method is foolhardy. Thus, leaving aside the feuds of various partisanships, we can say that any system, provided it is followed by talented men, has its own intrinsic probity.

The question now arises: which of the three picture planes (foreground, middleground, or background) should be held in *sharp,* and which in *soft* focus? This choice is also a matter of personal preference. These planes can all be treated uniformly in one way or another, or the treatment of the planes can differ. Assuming that we focus our eyes on distant areas, objects nearby may be indistinct; conversely, attention centered on the nearest objects may result in a "fade-out" of the distance. One lesson emerges here from these considerations: the painter, like the pianist who uses the pedals of his instrument, can intensify or soften contours as he sees fit; or as the situation warrants.

### ATMOSPHERIC PERSPECTIVE

In the preceding pages, I discussed the issues of linear perspective and the treatment of contours. There remains the problem of color, which is intimately connected with the appearance of objects placed on various planes of the picture.

Historically, it appears that changes in the intensity, hue, and value of color seen in the distance—and conditioned by *atmospheric perspective*—were recognized throughout the ages, although the same is not true of linear perspective. It is a common experience that colors fade in the distance. Even the most powerful hues, of red, yellow, and so forth will appear bluish when seen from far away. Hence the term, *atmospheric,* refers to the moisture in the air,

the vapors that account for color changes. Strong colors—called *local*—when placed on a distant plane, would destroy the illusion of distance, and thus run counter to the principles of atmospheric perspective. This premise applies mainly to the classic conception of the pictorial treatment of landscapes.

However, in a more modern system, such as encountered in the work of Cézanne, for example, different premises prevail. Deprived of their high chroma and thus lower in key, almost identical colors are used throughout the entire picture surface. Of course these pictures were never meant to show indefinite distance. Only foreground and middleground are considered; in the middleground, distance is always concealed behind a range of mountains, thus shutting off pictorial space midway. The contemporary artist—whether he follows classic, impressionistic or post-impressionistic doctrines, or is unconcerned with realistic representation—may use any conceivable colors, provided these nonconforming colors "work." Seeing this depends on personal ingenuity, because it is impossible to devise a formula for an unconventional approach.

### COLOR BALANCE

Another function of color in a composition is to balance the weight of masses distributed throughout the picture. No matter how well a picture is composed, the value and resonance of a particular color, placed in a particular location, may radically alter this balance. Even a small area of a high-keyed color can be powerful enough to tip the scale and outweigh a far *larger* area of a quieter, more neutral color.

However, a composition can be unbalanced not only by colors of high key, but by color density as well. Consider a shadow found on an object, or its cast shadow: the degree of the shadow's density will move the object forward, or push it into the background. Soft, transparent shadows, like veils, move objects back from nearby locations; dark shadows *keep* them in the forefront.

As I have previously mentioned, when you plan a picture, important elements of the com-

Figure 38  The format of a painting influences composition by promoting a certain distortion, or conditioning, of forms. Here, the emphasis is on horizontal arrangement; hence objects are stretched to fit their assigned space.

Figure 39  In this example, the emphasis is on verticality, calling for a corresponding change in the object's shape.

position should not be placed in corners or along borders where they will either tend to remain separate parts or prevent the viewer from becoming involved with the painting as a whole. The same principle applies to colors. When you place strong colors in the corners or along the borders, the viewer's attention will be distracted from the central interest of a picture.

### PICTURE FORMAT

In discussing the problems of composition, one important aspect remains: the shape of your canvas or panel. This shape will radically influence the nature of the composition. For instance, in Fig. 38, the horizontal format will condition the motifs to conform to its elongated space. In Fig. 39, the proportions are reversed; here, the motif will have to conform to the imposed verticality. In contrast, a square or approximately square canvas generally lacks any suggested direction; it will also be difficult to handle because the uniform relationship of height to width lacks *tension*.

These three shapes of canvas deviate from those sizes we have come to accept as standard stretcher sizes (and the corresponding frame sizes), stocked by art supply stores. These standard sizes are 10″ x 12″, 12″ x 16″, 20″ x 24″, 24″ x 30″, 30″ x 36″. Personally, I regard these proportions as somewhat "well-behaved," because the difference between their width and their height is moderate.

When they are well conceived, distortions condition the character of an object, endowing it with dramatic emphasis. However, a dramatic approach does not suit everyone; the more realistic a painter's conception, the less it will allow distortions. After all is said, the student should remember that successful painting does condition the character of an object, endowing not result either from willful coercion into the dramatic, or from blind faithfulness to natural appearances. In the end, everything depends upon a painter's native talent.

### DIVISION OF PICTORIAL SPACE

After you decide on the picture format, an

40A

40B

40C

40D

67

important concern will be where to place the horizon line, or, if this is not in evidence, the division between sky and land. In Fig. 40, graphic representation of such a division is given.

As shown in Fig. 40A, the equal division of land and sky will not work because all other elements of the composition, no matter how asymmetrical, will not be able to offset the unfavorable symmetry of the surface. In Fig. 40B, the "ideal" space division appears and is arranged according to the golden section; here the harmony between the sky and the land mass seem nearly perfect. But this ideal condition need not be taken too literally, for the extremes seen in Figs. 40C and 40D could prove just as desirable, or, in some instances, even preferable.

First let us consider carefully the situation exemplified in Fig. 40C. Here the horizon line is high up on the picture plane. Such an arrangement offers the painter an almost unlimited territory for developing his composition. Watching from a lofty position, the painter thus becomes a cartographer, as it were, mapping out vast vistas of land with all their complex configurations. Needless to say, this situation is the most difficult one to master; considerable knowledge of perspective and composition is needed to deal with such a large area.

It is interesting to recount the genesis of the system of pictorial visualization in Fig. 40C. In the Middle Ages, when landscape painting started to assert itself, and at once achieved a grandeur never surpassed (all this happened in Flanders), painters faced a break with tradition. And traditions, once established, were not discarded overnight; they endured over long periods of time, which allowed them to be developed and perfected.

Traditionally, medieval painting did not recognize the third dimension—instead, gold backgrounds were used in representations of biblical events. Hence, the first attempts at lifting the golden curtains were carried out reluctantly; a small aperture was created at the top of the panels to represent the area of the sky. In due course the horizon was placed lower, then still lower, reaching its lowest point in Dutch painting of the 17th century. Thus (as in Fig. 40D),

the sky assumed the dominant position. And what offers less complication than painting a sky, even one filled with complex cloud formations?

## LIGHT AND SHADE

Before you start a picture, remember that the interrelation of light and shade will not only materially influence coloristic effects, but this relationship will also help establish the character of the composition.

Emphasis and relaxation, point and counterpoint, can be worked out most effectively by means of the interplay of light and shade, thus creating definite rhythms in the architecture of the pictorial space. Well-considered use of light and shade can subdue one passage, activate another, and reduce or increase the intensity of a color. Notice how shadows deprive a color of its value by veiling it. This veil appears in landscapes as a bluish tint of varying intensity, depending on the nature of the light source and on the color of the object upon which the shadow falls. Hence, shadows are predominantly *cool,* even when cast upon hot sand.

## DISPERSED LIGHT

Two principal categories of lighting can be used in landscape painting: dispersed light and focal light. When light is dispersed, definite shadows are absent; for when light plays upon an object from all directions, the shadow itself and the cast shadow virtually cease to exist. In consequence, when you choose this type of illumination, the opportunity to display colors will be enhanced. However, these brilliant colors exist at the expense of the plasticity of objects; for it is the shadow proper and the cast shadow that make an object appear in the round.

However, dispersed light need not necessarily offer an opportunity for a display of colors. Certain conditions of dispersed light—such as we encounter after sunset, for example, or in a heavy overcast—would favor tonal values as well as color contrasts.

As for sunlight in painting, the Impressionists relied exclusively upon it. But the colored shadows which they used destroyed the solidity of their focus; hence their paintings appear as if seen in dispersed light. They called such lighting "plein air."

The impressionistic mode lasted for a generation. Its chief merit was a therapeutic effect on the understanding and use of color; for the first time color was employed for its own sake. Impressionism freed the murky palette of the 19th century academician from its "brown sauce," destroyed certain artificial taboos, and, in large measure, contributed to an enrichment of the painter's palette. However, the methods of the Impressionists now appear antiquated; in fact, these methods were already discarded by the Post-impressionists before the end of the 19th century.

## FOCAL LIGHT

Focal light, on the other hand, emanates from a definite source, such as the sun or sunlight issuing from an opening, as in a cloud bank. A light thus directed will create definite areas of light and shade on an object. There are three principal categories of focal light: light from above, light from the side, and *raking* light.

In landscape painting, the higher the light on the horizon, the more sober the mood of the scene, except when the light descends as a shaft on isolated areas. This mood of sobriety usually occurs because the sun, high in the sky, creates naturalistic effects, reduces the plasticity of objects, and deprives them of a romantic aura.

When the light enters the scene from the side, the plasticity—or roundness—of objects will be materially increased; they will also receive stronger emphasis.

Finally, the so-called raking light is created by a light source low on the horizon. Such illumination spells a romantic mood par excellence.

Whereas a light from the top may deprive the most exciting motif of its drama (just recall the relatively flat appearance of the Grand Canyon at noon), the light of the declining sun can glorify even a small pebble, lending it significance and making it appear singularly impressive. When an object casts a short shadow (at high noon), it tends to induce a feeling of drowsiness in us, but long shadows never fail to create an aura of nostalgia. Thus, noon time is the hour of prosaicism—the departing sun, an instrument of poetry.

It must be understood, however, that a device of illumination cannot be used at will to create a poetic mood. This particular lighting device (declining sun) has a long history behind it, and it has already congealed into a formula now used in commercial advertising. As always, the artist's talent, when authentic, will in the end decide whether his representations are convincing or not.

# CHAPTER 7

# Color mixing

I have stated that a good composition is the backbone of every painting. The issues of composition, if not successfully resolved, will invalidate any other virtues that a painting may have. Now we may ask: how about the colors? Will a poor disposition of colors also hurt other good qualities of a painting? Yes, "atrocious" colors will undoubtedly do this. But colors that are merely indifferent—colors that have little resonance—will not destroy the probity of the whole. In landscape painting, coloristic problems are more complex than those found in still life or figure painting because the great variety of motifs and the demands of atmospheric perspective complicate the landscape painter's task.

## CHARACTERISTICS OF COLOR MIXTURES

To acquaint yourself with the mixing properties of colors, first consider all the colors we shall have to place on our palette, either now or later.

*Flake white* cuts the intensity of all colors, re-ducing them to pastel hues. If too much white is added, the color mixture becomes chalky. Certain colors, if not used for glazing, will have to be mixed with white or some other heavy, opaque *body color* that will add substance to their transparency; these colors are *viridian green, phthalo blue* and *green, ultramarine blue, Hansa yellow,* and *alizarin crimson.*

*Ivory black:* with the exception of *Naples yellow,* this black will change all the yellows (and this includes all the *ochres, Mars yellow,* and *raw siena*) to greens. When black is mixed with *cadmium yellow,* the green is very intense. If white is added, you can get an endless variety of dull greens. Such gray-greens are indispensable for ground color in landscape, although not always suitable for foliage. Because black mixed with white yields a dull gray, a combination of any color with black and white will appear grayish. When *Mars black* is used, a cooler and still duller gray results.

*Prussian blue* is undoubtedly the most important blue for landscape painting. Its one-time bad reputation came from statements made by uninformed writers in obsolete textbooks. It can seldom be used when mixed with white alone because of the fierce hue of the blue; hence, to keep it in check, umber is always required. When mixed with yellows, Prussian blue produces the most brilliant greens. In fact, in mixtures with *cadmium yellow,* the green is so powerful that white is usually needed to soften its intensity.

With *Naples yellow* (and white), Prussian blue produces a very interesting, distant blue-green. When glazed with *burnt siena* over a yellow underpainting, the deepest transparent green appears. Other useful mixtures are: with *Venetian red* and white, a low-keyed purple; with *Mars violet* and white, a dark, powerful blue-violet. But primarily, Prussian blue is also indispensable for achieving grays. In combination with *umber* and white, an endless variety of grays can be produced in nuances that cannot be obtained from mixtures of other colors. (Without white, the mixture with umber will appear black.)

*Ultramarine blue* can be mixed with the same colors as *Prussian blue,* also with white without the admixture of *umber.* But with yellows, ultramarine yields weaker greens; with reds, a much higher-keyed purple; with umber (and white), grays with a slightly purplish cast; and with *viridian green* (and white), a beautiful range of blue-greens. The same mixtures can be made with *phthalo blue,* although the nuances of such combinations will differ from the former.

*Viridian green,* mixed with white alone, produces cool, "inorganic" greens, that is, not those usually seen in verdant matter. With *Naples yellow,* distant atmospheric greens can be obtained; with all the other yellows, a variety of dull greens. Viridian green is particularly suitable for mixtures with reds such as *Venetian red,* or *cadmium red* and white. Green and red, as we know, are complementary colors, one having the tendency to neutralize the other—that is, to reduce one another to grays. Hence, when green and red are mixed, greenish or pinkish grays will result, depending on the predominance of red or green.

*Phthalo green* will behave similarly, but the values obtained will be considerably stronger. This strength should not be considered an advantage; for a strong color is, more often than not, difficult to coordinate in a general color scheme.

*Chrome oxide green dull:* This dull hue can be made livelier by an admixture of any one of the *cadmium* colors. It handles beautifully with *Venetian red, Mars violet,* and black.

*Naples yellow,* with all the blues and viridian green (and white), produces bluish green atmospheric effects; lively pinks with *Venetian* and *cadmium red;* dull pink with *burnt siena;* and warm grays with *umber.*

*Ochre:* any of the stronger yellows—*zinc, strontium, Hansa,* or the *cadmiums*—will make ochre more brilliant; when mixed with *cadmium red* and white, a peculiar salmon pink results. Ochre will also brighten the hue of *burnt siena* and *umber.*

*Strontium and zinc yellows* are interesting in mixtures with *cadmium red.* However, their usefulness in combinations other than with the blues and *viridian green* will be quite limited in landscape painting.

*Cadmium yellows* will yield a brilliant orange when combined with *cadmium red,* and a dull orange when mixed with *Venetian red.* With *umber,* a dull but useful green can be obtained; with *alizarin crimson,* a brilliant purplish red identical with *cadmium red dark.*

*Hansa yellow* is suitable chiefly for glazing, and for tinting flake white when it is used in underpaintings.

Mixtures of the remaining colors with black were discussed at the beginning of this chapter. The last color on our palette, *alizarin crimson,* is the rarest to be used for landscape painting,

Arrangement of colors on palette.
Colors on the left hand side and
across the top are warm. Cold
colors are arranged on the right
hand side.

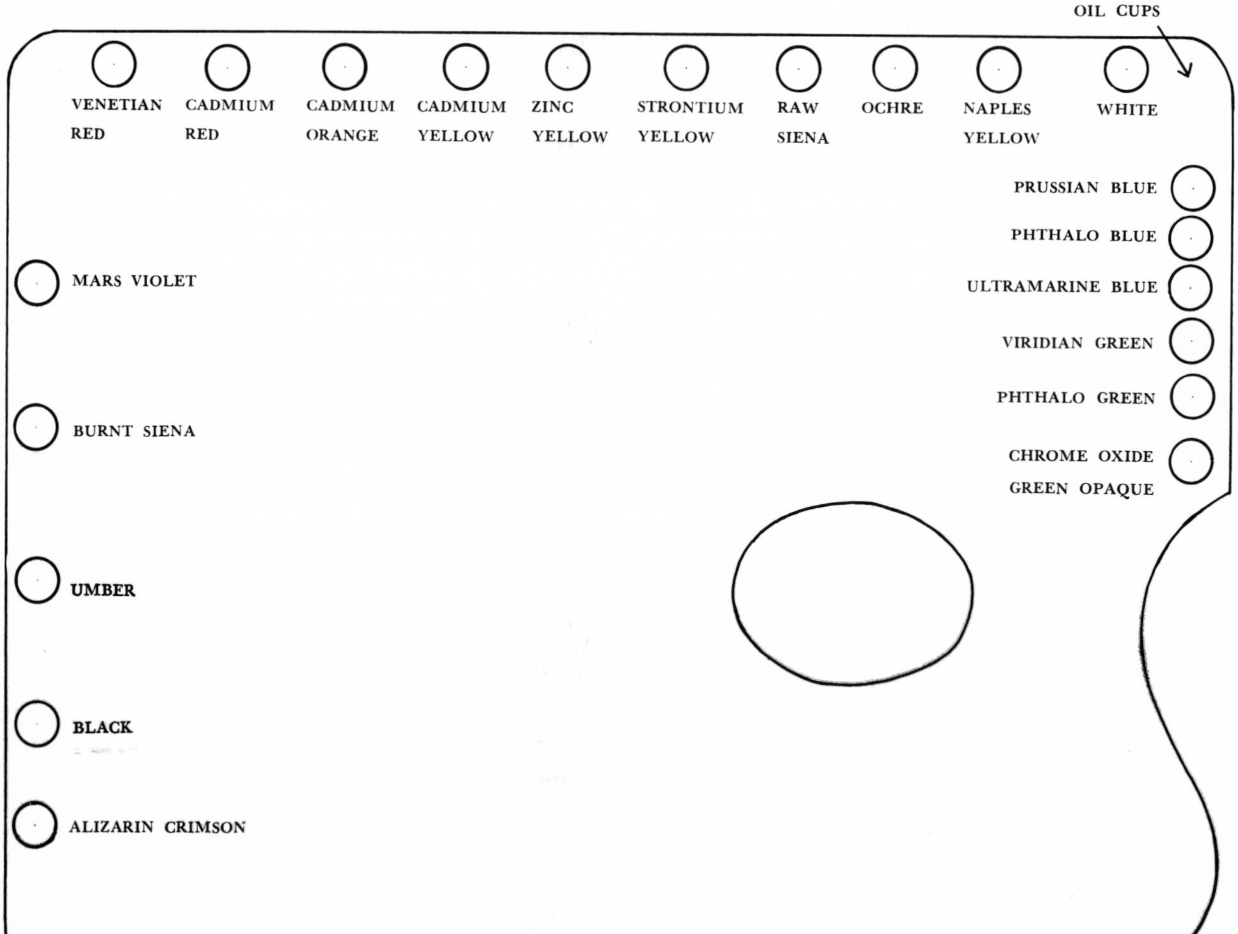

OIL CUPS

VENETIAN RED    CADMIUM RED    CADMIUM ORANGE    CADMIUM YELLOW    ZINC YELLOW    STRONTIUM YELLOW    RAW SIENA    OCHRE    NAPLES YELLOW    WHITE

PRUSSIAN BLUE

PHTHALO BLUE

MARS VIOLET

ULTRAMARINE BLUE

VIRIDIAN GREEN

PHTHALO GREEN

BURNT SIENA

CHROME OXIDE GREEN OPAQUE

UMBER

BLACK

ALIZARIN CRIMSON

except perhaps for flamboyant sunsets and for firelike effects, combined with *cadmium yellow*.

## COLOR MIXTURES FOR SPECIFIC PURPOSES

It is not only the beginner who may be baffled when he faces the choice of one color or another for a particular subject; even the most experienced artist may suffer from the same anxiety. Only in nonobjective art is the choice of colors (as well as the forms) entirely arbitrary. Here I shall review motifs found in nature and discuss the possibilities of coloristic treatment. Let us start first with the distant planes.

## CLEAR SKIES

The first color that comes to mind is, of course, blue. You have a choice of three blues: Prussian, phthalo, and ultramarine.

As I have mentioned, white and enough umber will have to be mixed with Prussian blue to tone down its aggressive hue. The value of this blue mixture will, of course, depend on the quantity of the "pacifiers" (white and umber) used. But regardless of the modification, a greenish cast will prevail. This greenish cast (which always seems agreeable) can be strengthened by adding Naples yellow or ochre. At times, even a trace of Venetian red could be combined with the mixture of Prussian blue and white, for warmer variances.

Secondly, consider phthalo blue. When sufficiently mixed with white, it will produce a blue which, for lack of a better term, I would call neutral. It is reminiscent of the celestial color of lapis lazuli, the ancient pigment of the old masters. It appears, however, that phthalo combined with a warm color, such as umber, yields a purplish hue, which I find unpleasant. A trace of ochre is all that I would add to this mixture to improve its value.

Ultramarine is the sweet, flowery blue we see in the placid skies of spring. Because ultramarine has a slight violet cast, umber is not the happiest choice as a modifying color. Ochre does better in this respect; viridian green is an excellent choice. In fact, ultramarine blue, viridian green, and white comprise the coloristic (if not chemical) equivalent of *cerulean blue*.

The latter is not on our list because it can be made through the intermixture I have mentioned; cobalt, another related blue, is also omitted because I find it rather superfluous. However, this is a matter of personal choice.

Thus far, I have been discussing a blue sky. But a sky may be ostensibly cloudless, yet fail to display the familiar blue. Vaporous atmospheric conditions can, under various light conditions, endow the sky with different colors. This area can be light-drenched, for example; in which case Naples yellow, white, and black, or strontium yellow, white, and black can be used, depending on the intensity of the yellow light. You can suggest a mellow, pre-sunset atmosphere by mixing cadmium red, viridian, and white to provide a cloudless sky of pink-green tonality.

Thus far, colors for clear skies have been discussed. They were: blues of every kind, yellows, and pink-greens. These seem to be practically all the color combinations that could be used successfully for this purpose.

## CLOUDS

As soon as clouds appear, they widen the range of colors that may enter the sky area.

First, for white, fleecy clouds—logically—mainly white will be used. As soon as white clouds assume bulk, light and shade will appear. While the light on such clouds may have a yellowish tinge, especially late in the day, it is questionable whether such coloristic effects can be used in contemporary painting without looking "picture-postcardish."

For the shadow on billowing clouds, two sets of colors can be used: Prussian, ultramarine, or phthalo blue with umber; or one of the same blues with burnt siena (white will always be part of all these mixtures). The painter should keep in mind that the warmer the color added to the blue (particularly to the violet-tinged ultramarine), the more purplish the color will appear. Hence, considering this rule, phthalo blue or ultramarine and burnt siena will provide a stronger purplish cast. When instead of burnt siena, Venetian or cadmium red is used, the purple becomes greatly intensified. To carry this to extremes, mixtures of ultramarine and alizarin crimson will account for an intense purple which, perhaps, could be used in a sunset—by painters who could handle such a condition with impunity.

Other color combinations for various delicate cloud effects are: Naples yellow, ultramarine, burnt siena; burnt siena and viridian green; viridian green and Venetian or cadmium red. White must be added to each of these mixtures.

In color combinations for strong cloud effects, white will be used to gray down and to reduce the powerful hues of the following mixtures: Prussian blue and Venetian red; chrome oxide green dull and Prussian blue; chrome oxide green dull and Mars violet; Mars violet and Venetian red.

Lastly, we shall touch again on a "dangerous" subject—the sunset sky, or rather clouds illuminated by the sun low on the horizon. Colors useful for such occasions are: Naples yellow, cadmium red, alizarin crimson, viridian green. In an emergency, one of the stronger yellows—strontium, zinc, or even cadmium yellow—could be used. But always keep in mind the pitfall that may lie ahead: the achievement of a flamboyant calendar illustration.

### THE HORIZON

Here we shall discuss colors of the most distant areas in a landscape, where the sky meets the ground. To begin with, one important point should be stressed: *if the color of the sky is darker than the ground, the horizon line comes forward.* Distance ceases to be infinite when the dark sky, like a curtain, shuts off our view at a certain point. Only when the light area of the sky meets the light area of the ground—only the confluence of both—will suggest the deepest penetration of space.

Another point to remember is that all distant colors must be mixed with white so that they will be opaque. Contrary to the beliefs of the inexperienced, glazes should not be used at distant planes because glazes come forward; they simply do not work in distances. Whether these distant colors are stronger or weaker—that is, receive more or less of the white—depends on

the kind of light and the nature of the clouds. But no matter what the motifs are, the following colors belong to the distance: ultramarine, phthalo, and Prussian blue; viridian green; Naples yellow—all mixed with white.

### MIDDLEGROUND AND FOREGROUND

In the middleground, the key of all colors will be higher, with less white in the intermixtures. The ochres, raw siena, and Mars yellow can be used instead of Naples yellow (besides the blues and viridian) ; if needed, black can be added to gray down the colors. We have mentioned two yellows which appear infrequently on the painters' palette: zinc and strontium. These are less aggressive colors that can be used very well in the middle distance, whereas cadmiums would be too strong—they would advance to the foreground.

Therefore, in the middle distance, the ground color will be greenish rather than bluish. The closer we move toward the foreground, the stronger colors will appear, ending finally in *local* colors—that is, colors not conditioned by atmospheric perspective. Such colors can be used—if the occasion allows—in full strength.

### CLASSICAL AND OTHER SYSTEMS

To pause for a moment, it should be said that the conditions described in the preceding paragraphs relate to classic painting, that is, to systems that consider atmospheric perspective and are generally concerned with natural appearances. Whenever a painter's subjective sensations enter, principles and systems cease to operate—and anything goes. Painting guided by the intention to be original, with reliance on purely emotional responses, will hardly produce great art or even good art. This kind of art, however, might find critical acclaim, especially nowadays when time-tested standards of value have been discarded.

Whether the painter's approach is realistic, expressionistic, or what have you, the validity of his presentation will depend entirely on his artistic potential. Suffice it to say that only the classic—that is, what has become a pragmatic certainty—can be taught; originality of expression cannot be attained by a calculated disregard of tradition.

## TREES

Since the color of trees is mainly green (blue-green, yellow-green), closely related colors would be used when trees appear in the background. If placed far enough in the distance, foliage would take on nearly the same color as its surroundings. These colors could be mixed from ultramarine, Naples yellow, and viridian green.

In the middleground, Prussian blue, ochre, zinc, or strontium yellow could be used; in the foreground, our strongest local greens.

Now we could ask, what about the autumn foliage? Here again we would find ourselves on treacherous ground; flamboyant fall foliage may quite easily place the work in the calendar category. Why? I suppose because these colors are too obvious—they do not allow a personal interpretation. Which colors would be suitable for this occasion? Burnt siena, cadmium orange, cadmium red, and cadmium yellow, and for the "daring" ones, perhaps a dash of alizarin crimson.

## ROCKS

As we know, rock color can have a broad range. However, these colors, like those of any object in landscape, will be affected by atmospheric perspective. Even the reddest rock will end up a faded blue-green on the distant plane. Also the middleground, as a rule, will not allow the presence of high-keyed colors.

Remember, though, that the painter should not be a slave of rules; he can deviate from the facts as seen in nature, provided he does it convincingly. So, for greater emphasis, a stronger color may be placed where it is not expected.

Moreover, natural phenomena often cannot be depicted exactly as they appear; for what may be attractive in nature may not be effective in a painting, or even altogether paintable. Hence, exotic colors of rocks, as seen in some regions of our Western desert, for example, should be left to the color photographers.

We may consider the following principal tonalities of rock masses. For the distance, bluish or yellowish gray. When seen from a closer vantage point, the general tone could be: gray-pink—burnt siena, black, and white; greenish gray—chrome oxide green dull, cadmium yellow, black, and white; bluish gray—Prussian blue, umber, and white; yellowish gray—umber, ochre, and white. Endless coloristic variations can be obtained, depending on the predominance of one or another color.

## WATER

It should be said that seascapes are not considered in this book, save where the sea is part of a landscape.

When we think of water, blue comes to our mind first; but it should be the last color to choose. Although we are not concerned with a purely naturalistic representation of the subject, let us note the conditions under which water appears blue. First, the sky must be blue, since the water mirrors it. Second, the surface of water must be smooth; any ripples would prevent the mirroring of the sky. Further, the area surrounding the body of water has a definite influence on its color. Lastly, color can be influenced by the mineral content of water. I know of a lake in Northwestern Canada where the water is emerald green; as far as I could ascertain, a mineral infusion is responsible for this brilliant color.

Often an inexperienced student will paint a brook in a heavily wooded or marshy surrounding in a brilliant blue. Now would there really be any glints of blue there? Usually, these blue tones would be overwhelmed by the preponderance of greens, and by the occasional wisps of white—the foam of rushing water. For example, what color should be given a waterfall? White, nothing but white.

When considering the choice of color for a body of water, your first consideration should be how the color harmonizes with the surrounding areas, not how accurately it approximates the particular image you remember. The most frequent objection a student makes to my criticism is: "But it *looks* exactly the way I painted it." Perhaps it does. But judged from an artistic point of view, it may be totally wrong. For example, on a light-colored expanse of land, a body of water may look much more interesting when kept dark, even very dark, although actually it reflects light and appears glistening white on much of its surface.

Let us now enumerate colors and color combinations which may be used to represent seas, rivers, streams, brooks, waterfalls, lakes, waterholes, even puddles: (1) white; (2) yellow; (3) very light pink (yes, there are situations where pink water may be just right); (4) viridian green and white; (5) viridian green, Prussian blue, and white (in this instance I would not use any other blue which lacks the greenish cast of Prussian—the best blue for painting water); (6) viridian green, ochre, and white; (7) viridian green, ochre, Prussian blue, and ochre; (8) viridian green, ochre, black, and white (with or without a touch of Prussian blue); (9) and finally, our old standbys, Prussian blue, umber, and white—for all shades of warm grays, cold grays, slate grays, blue grays, blues, and just plain neutral grays.

### GENERAL OBSERVATIONS

Thus far, we have dealt with the principal motifs found in nature: skies, fields (ground), mountains (rocks), trees, water. What other elements are part of a landscape? Dwellings, people, animals, and many other objects. Now you may ask: how could I treat such incidental motifs? The answer can be found in the works of the great old masters.

From the study of the old masters' landscape paintings, we can see that man-made objects and man himself remain, most frequently, incidental motifs. These motifs are so minimized that their absence would in no way impair the composition. Of course, I am referring here only to *landscapes,* not to paintings where figural subjects have received a landscape background.

In my own landscapes, strongly influenced by the work of the early Flemish and German masters, the human presence is so minuscule that it does not register its presence in reproductions. The biblical titles I sometimes give to such paintings (like those from the Flemish school) serve merely for identification purposes. It would seem that when a landscape is conceived on what we may call a heroic scale, human presence dwindles into insignificance. Hence, in such a landscape, placing a character dressed in blue jeans, a ten gallon hat, and so on, would be absurd.

Could we use a regional motif—a barn, a cow, etc.—in a landscape? Indeed, a landscape can illustrate a particular environment. But the difficulty will be how to avoid making the picture a mere illustration. Is *mere illustration* a negative assessment? It is, inasmuch as the aim and the objective of an illustration is, first and last, storytelling. Here, every element of the scene and all its actors are of prime importance, no matter how much these elements may run counter to artistic needs. How can one circumvent this difficulty and still retain a landscape's particular character? This can be done in a rather elegant manner, described in the section, "Open Color Painting," in Chapter 9.

# CHAPTER 8

# Glazes and scumbles

Before I discuss specific techniques of painting a landscape, the mechanics of paint application must be understood. Paint application, if done for artistic ends, involves the achievement of what called as *paint quality.* I referred to this problem earlier, and asserted that it concerns the quality of brushstrokes, texture, and contours. These distinctions may seem theoretical, but they become clearer when we compare a painting made by an unskilled hand with a master's work. The first will have no paint quality, but the master painting will demonstrate it in full measure.

Brushstrokes may, or may not, be skillful; they may be meaningful and personal, or perfunctory and without character. Texture, as well as treatment of contours, can be varied and sensitive or merely indifferent. Let us consider texture first, as it is created by glazes and scumbles.

## GLAZING

A thin, transparent film of color (greatly di- luted by the medium) which reveals the underlying color, is referred to as a glaze. *The underlying color must always be opaque, and lighter than the superimposed, transparent color.* Hence, glazes have a luminous appearance, for it is the light from within that imparts luminosity to a paint film. The lighter an underlying color, the more effective will be the glaze, provided a strong color was used for glazing. Weak tints are not suitable for this purpose.

Colors useful for glazing in landscapes are (from lightest to darkest): ochre, Hansa yellow, raw siena, Mars yellow, cadmium yellow, viridian green, phthalo green, burnt siena, umber, black. A narrow most suitable range will be limited to: viridian green, ochre, Hansa yellow, burnt siena. *Never mix white with a glazing color,* for white destroys its transparency.

As I have mentioned, glazing with a brush can be done only on a *perfectly dry surface.* But when you use a knife—and great skill—you can glaze even a wet (viscous) surface. You can use glazes while in the process of painting; or a finished, dry painting can be glazed to make a passage more colorful, or to dim it.

To a large extent, the appearance of glazes is influenced by the texture of the underlying support. If this texture is purposely rough—due to an impasto—so much the better. But underlying surfaces with *accidental* textures may ruin the character of a glaze. An uninteresting mechanical grain or a conspicuous grain of the canvas will do the same. Therefore, when using canvas, remember that a carefully prepared underpainting is essential for the proper effect of a glaze. A gesso ground on a panel will always be suitable for this purpose.

As I mentioned, the paint used for glazing must be strongly diluted with the medium. In fact, it should be as thin as watercolor. Obviously, such paint has little body of its own; hence, to act well, it must be properly conditioned. First, mix each half inch of the color, as it comes from the tube, with a little of the Copal Concentrate. Scoop the concentrate out of the wide-mouthed bottle; then, thoroughly mix the paint with as much copal as the tip of the painting knife holds. As you shall realize at

once, a certain transformation of the paint body occurs; it becomes unctuous, pliable, viscous. It flows more easily; it attaches itself to the surface more firmly; its body gains firmness, and besides, the color takes on greater lustre.

However, as we know, the concentrate is not a paint *thinner,* but merely a paint modifier. To thin the paint, use Copal Painting Medium Heavy because this is more viscous than the one designated *Light*. All this serves to improve the adhesive properties of the thin paint material, to prevent its dripping down from the upright support, and to insure permanence of the painting.

Glazing is a one-time operation. A color once glazed cannot be improved by subsequent glazing, although it could be dimmed, that is, made less active. Glazing is an operation planned in advance. It cannot be done during the process of painting, at any odd time, unless the surface has been prepared for this purpose. Hence, in improvised painting, glazes will appear but rarely. When your painting method employs a series of overpaints, glazing will usually be ex-

41A

41B

41C

cluded. In alla prima painting (see next chapter), glazes will predominate. (Glazes are not represented by a color chart because they do not register in print.)

### HARD RESINS IN GLAZES

I cannot too strongly impress upon the student the inadvisability of using a soft resin medium such as a mixture of damar, turpentine, and linseed oil. Glazes are exceedingly vulnerable; when compounded with a medium that remains forever soluble under the mildest paint solvents, their future cleaning without injury to the paint film is quite problematic, if not impossible. This is not to say that paint greatly diluted even with the copal medium could withstand *forceful rubbing* with a strong paint solvent; but its permanence will be comparable to that found on the best preserved paintings by the old masters.

It should be known that atmospheric dirt will attach itself to a paint film sooner or later, depending on local conditions in city or country. Substances like tobacco smoke, volatilized grease from kitchens, etc., will settle on the picture's surface, obscuring its appearance to a lesser or greater extent. In my own experience, thinly executed passages on paintings done with soft resin medium in the studio of Max Doerner (my teacher at one time) proved quite impermanent when examined more than forty years later. Hence the importance of hard resin.

### SCUMBLING

As I mentioned, only in alla prima painting is the surface always ready to accept glazes. In other instances, glazing cannot very well be improvised. Scumbling, on the other hand, can be done at any time; for improvised painting, it is the method par excellence.

What is a scumble? It is the reverse of a glaze: namely, *a semi-transparent, light color passage resting on top of a darker surface.* While we can say that glazing is related to watercolor painting, scumbling is intrinsically an oil painting technique. It relieves dark, opaque areas of gloom and dullness; and, if skillfully used, it

produces liquid effects of light.

To illustrate, compare a light, semi-opaque color, painted over a light surface, with the same light color painted over a dark surface. In the first instance, the color passage will prove to be entirely ineffective; while in the second, the sensation of light will be strong and incisive. (Scumbling is demonstrated in Fig. 41.)

What kind of colors are used for scumbling? Any color from our list will be suited for this purpose, but most of them will have to be mixed with white—just the opposite of what we do in glazing. As I have said, you must apply a scumble upon a dark surface. Dark is, of course, a relative value: a light gray will be dark in comparison with white. Therefore, a scumble is possible even on a light gray surface provided that a lighter color is used on top if it—white, for instance. However, the darker the underlying tone, the more brilliant a light scumble will appear. Hence, only dense colors such as ochres, yellows, and light red can be applied to a very dark surface without the admixture of white.

Conditioning paint with Copal Concentrate is just as important in scumbling as it is in glazing because, in scumbling, viscosity of paint is essential.

### THREE KINDS OF SCUMBLES

Let us look once more at Fig. 41A. Scumbling is least effective where a thin wash is brushed on, or applied with a painting knife to a dark surface moistened by the painting medium. It is important to mention that, before you begin to paint, you should *always brush or rub some of the painting medium into the surface,* to facilitate the application of paint and to assure better adhesion.

In Fig. 41B, a glaze (it can be any desirable color) was spread on the surface; then, the scumble was swept into the *wet glaze* with a painting knife. What are the advantages of such a procedure? The glaze imparts its own color to the scumble, thus enriching it. Moreover, the scumble will "sit" better in the film of the glaze. (To avoid misunderstanding, we have qualified a glaze as an application of a darker color on a lighter surface. However, even if a glaze is applied to a dark surface—therefore becoming invisible—it is still a glaze whose color will serve our purpose in scumbling.)

In Fig. 41C, instead of a glaze, a solid film of *appreciably thick paint* received a scumble applied with a painting knife. To do this successfully, the underlying wet paint must be sufficiently *viscous* to resist a tool working over it. A bristle brush, for example, could not be used very well for this purpose because its harsh bristles would dig into the soft paint rather than deposit the scumble on the surface. An elastic painting knife is a much more efficient tool for this purpose. Scumbles carried out in this manner are most effective, and most frequently used.

I mentioned that scumbles, unlike glazes, do not require a specially prepared surface, since scumbling is done wet-in-wet. In fact, any light surface can be turned into a dark one through overpainting, and scumbling can follow this overpainting, wet-in-wet.

# CHAPTER 9

# *Alla prima painting*

There are two principal methods of painting: the so-called *alla prima* technique, and painting on an underpainting, which I will discuss in the next chapter.

Alla prima is a one step operation. That is, the painting is done wet-in-wet; you aim from the start to produce final effects. This implies that a painting must be finished in a day, since, by the next day, the paint surface would be dry (our medium being fast drying) and a wet-in-wet painting would not be feasible. This one phase operation has one limitation: it excludes large works and those where a great amount of detail is involved. Moreover, large works, as a rule, do not look right when painted thinly; alla prima painting must, of necessity, be thin. Considering these factors, I would limit the size of an alla prima painting to no more than 16″ x 20″.

As to the support, gesso panels are best because their relatively smooth surface (or rather the lack of surface texture commonly present on canvas) does not resist the rapidly moving brush. In other words, such a smooth surface allows immediate realization of the painter's intentions. For this reason, *very smooth* canvas can also be employed for alla prima work. Before discussing this technique, it is of interest to review its history briefly.

### HISTORY OF ALLA PRIMA TECHNIQUE

The first major alla prima works appeared in early 16th century Flemish art. Hieronymus Bosch and Pieter Brueghel painted predominantly in this technique. Later, Rubens used it almost exclusively in his small panels, done entirely by his own hand. His sketchy technique appears quite *modern;* its kinship to some 19th and 20th century works is apparent. The work of the earlier Flemish masters, which were done on a large scale, look archaic, and do not appear thin at all; here, the wealth of detail and the Gothic narrative style account for the extraordinary richness of the artists' representations. All these paintings were done on wooden panels, in stages, which means that only certain areas of the panel were finished at one time. Of course, some contemporary painters may enjoy working in stages—to piece together a painting from many parts, as it were. Proceeding in this manner, they may, nevertheless, achieve a uniform effect.

The advantages offered by the alla prima method were recognized early. Before 1700, the Dutch painter and author, Van Mander, wrote an accurate account of the technique. Although alla prima work appears sporadically after this date, the orthodox or correct procedure, like many other traditional techniques, was generally forgotten.

### CHARACTERISTICS OF THE TECHNIQUE

The most striking characteristics of an alla prima painting are its freshness and sketchiness; such a painting lacks elaborations and all the cumbersome attributes of works which are painstakingly executed. The most salient observation about alla prima procedure was made by Van Mander; he stated that "much of the original painting ground remained uncovered and stood for final effects."

Now, exploitations of various painting grounds—to influence the final effects—appear frequently in many kinds of painting. Characteristically, in alla prima, there is evidence of the original *imprimatura,* a layer of *transparent color* applied to a white ground. In works of the Flemish masters (according to Van Mander's correct observation), this imprimatura, quite often, was flesh color. In the small panels by Rubens, much of the imprimatura is visible, and the drawing done on top of it remains evident in many places.

To sum up, the alla prima method relies on sketchy presentation. The *linear* element in the painting is particularly important; hence the scriptliner and round sable brushes should be used in preference to other tools. The painting knife will be employed only on occasion, because it does not work well on a rigid surface. To retain the character of this technique, glazes should be used more often than opaque applications; equally important, evidence of the imprimatura should remain preserved in many places of the panel. I do not stress these requirements merely because of some arbitrary orthodoxy, but because the intrinsic charm of the technique will not come to the fore unless these orthodoxies, or rules, are observed.

### FIRST STEP – DRAWING

The preparation of the panel was discussed in Chapter 1 on materials. Now, on top of the gesso, the drawing can be done with any desired graphic material: charcoal, pencil, crayon, India ink, or even pastel. The amount of drawing used—mere indications or more accurate elaborations—depends upon the painter's predilections. When finished, the drawing should be made permanent by means of a fixative.

Nowadays, most of the fixatives are made of a material which is turpentine resistant. If this were not the case, the drawing would be dissolved by any painting medium containing turpentine. You can prepare an adequate fixative yourself by dissolving one part (by weight) orange shellac in twelve parts wood alcohol. I have referred to the drawing made on white gesso; however, you can draw just as well on top of the imprimatura.

### SECOND STEP – IMPRIMATURA

Imprimatura, as mentioned, is a transparent color applied on top of the gesso (or on any white ground), since the white of the support must first be conditioned in some manner before it is painted upon.

With Bosch, burnt siena and ochre were the chief colors used for this purpose (hence Van Mander's reference to the "color of flesh"). Brueghel used similar colors, but in many of his works one can detect a pale yellow and a bluish gray. In Rubens, the imprimatura is very much in evidence, and its color range is extensive.

The purpose of the imprimatura is to create a general tone that will unify the final tonality of the entire painting. Since the color of the imprimatura remains visible in many parts of the finished panel, frequently asserting itself through the superimposed glazes, its importance cannot be overemphasized.

As I have said, the imprimatura is a *trans-*

*parent* color applied on top of the gesso. To achieve this transparency, any color—even the most opaque—can be *made* transparent *when it is sufficiently diluted by a medium.* The only appropriate medium for this purpose is the copal varnish previously described. A soft resin varnish (damar or a mastic) cannot be used for an imprimatura, which would be dissolved by the turpentine contained in the copal medium in subsequent paint applications.

Linseed oil would be entirely unsuitable for an imprimatura, because according to the principles of sound technique, painting should proceed from lean to fat. That is, initial layers of paint should be less oily than subsequent ones. A linseed oil imprimatura would introduce an oil saturated film at the very beginning.

Although, as I mentioned, almost any color can be used for an imprimatura, only a few should be selected. In landscape painting, our list will include one of the following: viridian green, ochre, Hansa yellow, cadmium yellow, burnt siena, and umber. Of course, as we know, every painter has to make his own choice of colors. White is the only color which should *never* enter a mixture prepared for an imprimatura, for the inherently opaque white would ruin its requisite transparency.

After diluting the chosen color, or colors, to the consistency of watercolor with copal varnish, apply the mixture all over the panel with a bristle brush in any desired manner: smoothly, in streaks, or even in blotches. Of course, you can proceed in a definite way, guided by the existing motifs drawn on the panel, applying differently colored imprimaturas to different motifs. This method is referred to as *multicolored imprimaturas,* discussed in this chapter.

It should be noted, however, that very light imprimaturas are ineffective; and very dark ones are difficult to handle and cannot be glazed. Dark imprimaturas will also hide the drawing made on the gesso. Generally speaking, a middle tone is best. It takes at least three days for the imprimatura to solidify to the degree where it becomes fairly resistant to the action of the turpentine contained in the painting medium.

Once the imprimatura is dry (it rapidly becomes dry to the touch), the drawing can be done very well on top of it and then fixed in the usual way. Since, in practice, many panels are prepared at one time for future use, you will often find yourself drawing on the *imprimatura,* rather than on the white gesso.

### THIRD STEP – GLAZING

Thus far, the following steps have been taken. A drawing was executed on the white gesso and rendered permanent by means of fixative. The chosen color for the imprimatura has been diluted by the copal varnish and spread on the gesso panel (or the drawing was made on top of the imprimatura and then fixed). Now, because the imprimatura film is on top, the gesso has become nonabsorbent to the degree required for oil painting. The imprimatura has been allowed to dry for at least three days.

At this point you may begin painting, but not before you mix all your colors on the palette with Copal Concentrate, and provide your oil cup with Copal Painting Medium Heavy. The choice of these materials is quite important in alla prima painting. For, as previously stated, a requisite viscosity and a heavy body of paint are *imperative in a technique that employs a lot of glazing.*

Before you start to paint, thinly cover the imprimatura with the painting medium (*before* painting, always rub some medium onto the paint surface), or mix the medium with some color (never with white or mixtures containing white). When I say *some* color, I mean just enough to produce a glaze. (A point to remember: when a color is mixed with *varnish* to a thin consistency, we refer to it as *imprimatura;* when the medium is used for this purpose, we call it a *glaze.*)

Oiling—applying a thin layer of medium— will not influence the color of the imprimatura except to make it deeper and more lustrous; but a glaze will change and often materially *enhance* its original color. For example, let us assume that the color of the imprimatura is derived from burnt siena. Glazing it with burnt siena will intensify the original color. But when you glaze the original burnt siena with viridian, a dark grayish tone will result. Here are a few

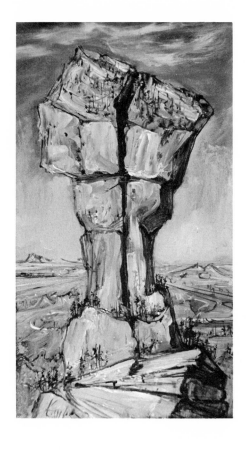

Figure 42 *The Rock* (7″ x 14″). The panel carries an imprimatura of ochre, while a darker tone of raw siena was applied to the rock and the ground area. Bristle brush, scriptliner, and painting knife were used—the knife only on the rock part. Glazes appear chiefly in the top part of the sky and the shadow side of the rock. In this painting, a shift in perspective was used to make the top of the rock appear as if seen from above, but the bottom part appears as if viewed from below.

combinations; many more can be worked out.

| Imprimatura | Glaze |
|---|---|
| ochre | ultramarine |
| cadmium or Hansa yellow | viridian |
| cadmium or Hansa yellow | burnt siena |
| burnt siena | phthalo green |
| burnt siena | viridian green |
| viridian green | burnt siena |

The most important thing to remember in glazing is that the *lighter* the color of the imprimatura and the *darker* and *thinner* the color of the glaze, the more luminous is the effect. It must be understood that in oil painting, the sensation of luminosity comes only from within, and can be attained only through glazes.

### COMPLETING THE PAINTING

I have thus far discussed all the steps preparatory to painting, and now to the painting proper (Fig. 42).

Size of the panel: 7″ x 12″. Priming: Liquitex gesso on Masonite. Drawing: charcoal on white gesso, made permanent by means of a fixative (here and there, the marks of the charcoal remain in evidence on the finished painting). Imprimatura: ochre. Glaze: raw siena. Range of colors (all compounded with Copal Concentrate): Prussian blue, viridian green, ochre, strontium yellow, burnt siena, umber. Medium: Copal Painting Medium Heavy. Brushes: striper and scriptliner; the painting knife was used only on the rock area. The painting was done into the wet glaze, and the chief accents rest on delineations. Much of the original imprimatura remains visible. The actual drawing and painting took less than two hours. Other examples of work in alla prima techniques are seen in Figs. 43 and 44.

A reminder concerning the size of the panel: although, as I mentioned, small panels are preferable, some painters, working on a large scale, may very well proceed in piecemeal fashion and finish certain areas of a painting at different times. Under normal circumstances, one cannot expect that the paint will still be wet the next day; hence, fresh paint cannot be

Figure 43A  *The Coast* (6″ x 9″). Other examples of alla prima painting are seen here and in *The Mountain View* (Fig. 44). *The Coast* is a miniature replica of the rather large painting reproduced in Fig. 8A but it is by no means treated in a miniaturistic manner. On the contrary, in spite of its small format, the delineations made with a scriptliner and striper are incisive, as are the marks of the knife on the central motif and on the left side of the foreground. An attempt was made to treat this little panel as if it were a painting of considerable size.

**Figure 44** *The Mountain View* (12″ x 16″). This painting received an imprimatura of cadmium yellow. Here, the entire painting (with the exception of a few small spots) consists of glazes—transparencies and semi-transparencies. The thin, liquid paint allowed a predominantly linear treatment. In fact, the entire painting is an essay in drawing with low-keyed colors; the luminous quality is provided by the radiant yellow imprimatura.

blended into the dry areas painted a day before.

For outdoor painting, the imprimatura method is ideal, inasmuch as rapid progress can be made, almost as in watercolor. The panel should carry an ochre imprimatura; this color is easy to handle and is well suited for painting any conceivable landscape motif.

### VARNISHING AND CORRECTIONS

Alla prima painting done in the described manner does not require varnishing for at least several years, and often for a very long time, since it dries with a gloss. The amount of Copal Concentrate and heavy medium in the paint will create a tough, nonporous paint film.

In case of failure, either discard the panel, or remove the dry paint from the surface. When some retouching and corrections appear necessary on a *finished* painting, the heavy paint should be smoothed out with a fine carborundum paper. Copal varnish should then be brushed over the sanded surface and allowed to solidify for about one hour. On older paintings, this procedure is not necessary; here, the repaints will dry with a gloss *matching* the gloss of the original painting, provided they have enough heavy medium and concentrate incorporated in them. Again, before you apply color for retouching, always rub some of the medium onto the surface to be overpainted.

### MULTICOLORED IMPRIMATURA

Thus far, I have been referring to the use of uniform colors for the imprimatura, that is, either one or a combination of several of the colors mentioned. However, several colors can be used *independently* on the same surface. This, in essence, is similar to the use of a multicolored underpainting, to be discussed in Chapter 10. Let us assume that our landscape composition combines the following motifs: sky, ground, and trees. In this case, we may vary the imprimatura color: for the area of the sky, burnt siena; for the ground, viridian green; and for the trees, ochre or some stronger yellow.

When discussing the application of the imprimatura, I mentioned that its color can be streaky, blotchy, or whatever one may choose. It need not be perfectly uniform. On the contrary, mechanically uniform color is tedious to the eye. In multicolored imprimatura, there is no need to unite and blend the various color areas nicely. An irregular application will in no way adversely affect the final appearance of the painting.

### ALLA PRIMA PAINTING ON TONED GROUND

For our purpose, the ground will either be light gray or light yellow. It is best to prepare the gray tone from Prussian blue, umber, and white; for the yellow color, mix ochre and white. The ground should be applied with a palette knife to the white priming of the canvas, so that *its tooth may largely disappear under the layer of paint.*

Prepared in this manner, the canvas becomes suitable for alla prima painting. Work done in this technique was quite common in 18th century Holland. However, the appearance of these paintings differs considerably from the alla prima work done on imprimatura: they do not possess luminous glazes because the white priming disappears completely under the superimposed toned ground. Hence, there is no evidence of the characteristic light from within, which only a gesso ground can provide. This circumstance does not make the technique inferior; it is merely responsible for different effects.

On a toned ground, instead of glazes, scumbles and opaque passages predominate because white is used to a much larger extent than in alla prima painting on an imprimatura. As always, the greatest advantage of painting on canvas is the opportunity to use a painting knife freely. Also, on a finished painting, corrections can be made more easily. Even complete overpainting can be done if desired; in this case, however, the alla prima character of the treatment would be lost.

### STEP-BY-STEP PROCEDURE

As stated, when you paint alla prima on toned ground, the canvas chosen should have very little tooth. Since, as a rule, not much impasto

appears on these paintings, the character of the fabric will remain evident on many areas of the picture. Therefore, it is advisable to use linen canvas rather than cotton, because, as we know, linen has a much more attractive texture.

(1) As suggested above, the toned ground is applied on top of the dry priming of the canvas. Depending on the subject matter chosen, a low-keyed yellow or a light gray ground should be used, or perhaps some other color. If greens predominate in the painting, a yellow ground is preferable. The ground should dry for at least a week.

(2) Draw the composition on the ground with charcoal, and then apply fixative. If preferred, the composition can be first developed on paper and then transferred to the canvas (for transfer paper, see Chapter 2 on materials).

(3) Oil the toned ground with Copal Painting Medium, using a brush. If *trickling* occurs, turpentine should first be brushed on freely, and then allowed to dry. Trickling—also referred to as *crawling*—refers to contraction of the medium on the surface of a painting, similar to the way water does on a piece of glass. The reason for this problem is not well understood, but the turpentine treatment is the best cure for it.

(4) Next you can concentrate on painting; should you plan to extend your working period over more than one day, avoid using quick-drying colors such as umber, burnt siena, Prussian blue, and all the Mars colors.

Unless the toned ground has first dried for several weeks, the finished painting will, upon drying, show dull spots, or it may become dull throughout. Remember, the more Copal Painting Medium Heavy and the concentrate, the glossier the painting.

However, the occurrence of dullness can be considered normal. It is caused by the under-layer of paint which, if not completely dry, will absorb some of the medium and the pigment's vehicle (linseed oil). Also, the slower the drying

◄ Figure 45A *Temptation of St. Anthony* (12″ x 16″). Light orange was chosen for the toned ground to influence the planned final color of the fantastic sandstone mass of the principal motif. It was obvious that a burnt siena glaze would provide the desired final color. A thin glaze was applied over the entire surface of the rock; next, the glaze was made darker (by adding a little black) to render the effect of shade; and, finally, the knife removed the glaze from parts that were to remain light. Now the reader might ask two questions. It has been mentioned that a horizon line should never be placed in the middle of the picture; but here it runs through the middle, and works well. The reason for this seeming contradiction is that the line is interrupted at irregular intervals, and the shapes of the rock in the upper part of the picture are so capricious that they do not allow the unfavorable division to assert itself. As to the second question, where is St. Anthony hiding? The title of the picture—like all my titles—is not important. Titles are given merely for identification purposes. But to legitimize it, the figure of the saint *was* placed in the picture; the reader is invited to locate it.

Figure 45B  As you can see from this detail, some of the glaze remained imbedded in the grain of the fabric, creating a variegated texture. With the exception of the sky, painted with the knife, only a round sable brush and a scriptliner were used. ▼

process, the more chance that the liquid constituent of paints will settle in the lower layer of the paint film, thus bringing a dull appearance of the linoxyn (dried film of oil paint). Of course, the situation is easily remedied—varnishing will do it at once.

In Fig. 45, *The Temptation of St. Anthony* (12″ x 16″), the work was done on a toned ground of pale orange, thin enough to reveal the fine texture of the linen fabric.

### OPEN COLOR PAINTING

First the definition: *open color,* as the term indicates, refers to the color (or colors) that go beyond the outer edges of an object. In contradistinction, a *closed color* is contained within an object's edges. Painting in open color is related to alla prima painting in two respects: reliance on the linear approach, and the one step operation. Open color painting cannot be improved by overpaints, although the passage can be restated later on, in conjunction with any technique subsequently used.

I mentioned that open color is a valuable method in dealing with marginal objects in a landscape; this method makes animate or inanimate objects appear incidental, by reducing their weight and incisiveness. In Figs. 46 and 47, the method is shown in two characteristic examples.

Before discussing the technique of open color painting, we will consider its implications more closely. Historically, the method is not a modern discovery, for we find it in the work of some 16th century painters. Even then, it served to simplify certain problems, and to save the painter from irrelevant details.

Let us consider, for example, painting the tiny head of a small figure which is part of a much larger composition. What kind of picture would the artist have if he elaborated on the head as follows: blond hair, blue eyes, cherry red lips, and perhaps pink cheeks. Altogether, it would amount to a pictorial nightmare. In certain early periods (the Gothic, for example), this could have been done with impunity. In our time, however, doing this would end in failure.

So, how can such a situation be handled in an esthetically acceptable manner? By using the same color (in this instance, a brownish red) for *drawing* all the features, you simplify the tedious miniaturistic process, and minimize the emphasis on marginal objects in the painting.

Let us consider another example: in a vast expanse of a landscape, there is a dwelling, or a group of dwellings, somewhere in the middleground. How often have I seen a student trying to paint the windows with all the glass panes neatly in place and differentiated in color from the rest of the house—indeed a feat of futility! Unless the student had decided, for some good reason, to paint a miniature, the following simple measure should be taken: the presence of the windows could be indicated by means of sketchy lines drawn on the color of the wall itself. In other words, the color of the windows would participate in the color or colors of the wall. These are typical occasions when the **open color technique** can be of great advantage.

From the above, it appears that the technique is very simple, since it relies chiefly on drawn lines. But here we have a problem: the procedure calls for a deft hand, for the drawn lines are made while painting into a wet color.

Now the question arises: why should the lines be drawn into a *wet,* and not onto a dry, paint layer? It would appear that dry paint would be much easier to paint on. Then, if corrections were needed, the drawing could be simply wiped off the dry surface and another attempt made. When painted into a wet paint layer, however, an unsatisfactory line would have to be removed with the underlying painting. In the end, this would result in a patchy appearance.

Why then do we *not* choose the first procedure and draw the lines on dry paint? The answer is that the superimposed lines would appear detached when painted on a dry surface, and would not become an integral part of the whole; in short, they would appear alien in the ensemble. On the other hand, when you paint wet-in-wet, there is always a certain confluence between the line and the adjoining surface. In fact, even some blending can be carried out judiciously here and there to weaken the effect of a line or to make it one with the surface.

Figure 46 In this demonstration, the character of the open color procedure is seen in a few objects: principally in the figures, tree trunks, and buildings. These objects are treated chiefly by outlines; their color is largely that of their backgrounds.

**Figure 47** In this detail from an alla prima painting, the area of the mountains is transparent: it allows you to see the ground and the sky behind it. A similar treatment is given to the sketchy figures. In contrast to the example in Fig. 46, these motifs are too small (the actual size of the figure in front is 1½″) to be given their own color; hence, the reliance on outlines. In the background, these outlines are greenish blue of varying intensities; the objects placed in front received dark delineations.

# CHAPTER 10

# Painting on an underpainting

What is an underpainting? It is a layer of paint that underlies the final, that is, the top surface of paint. Hence, an underpainting can be either a corrective layer hiding some initial unsuccessful attempt, or it can be purposeful; that is, it can enhance both *texture* and *color* of the final painting.

Theoretically, there is no exact number of underpaintings that should be used. You can use as many as you require to achieve the desired result. You may wonder in what way the *many* underpaintings aid the final appearance of the painting. As I have mentioned, they can create textures and add substance to the body of paint; but remember that the final color can only be influenced by the *last underpainting.*

*Texture* refers to the configuration of a picture's surface; it is nothing but a picture's topography, if we may say so. Texture is a very important quality in oil painting because it can greatly contribute to the sensual, that is, visual interest of a painting surface. Although, from the time of the Renaissance, painters tried to imitate the textures of objects closely—silk, fur,

stone, wood, and so forth—such exact duplication will not be our task. For we, as it appears, are enamoured of texture for its own sake: for the tactile and optical sensations it offers. But this is not to say that rendering the feel of an object's outer skin, as it were, is a transgression against some esthetic principles.

Before starting to discuss the step-by-step procedure of underpainting in impasti, a few cardinal rules should be mentioned.

(1) *Oiling between the layers of an underpainting is superfluous* because, at this stage of painting, the fluency of brush strokes is not important. However, before the *final* phase of painting —or at least one that is supposed to be final (this cannot always be previsualized with certainty)—the painting medium should be rubbed into the surface.

(2) Copal Concentrate need not be mixed with the paint because the richness of the paint body, the improved fusibility (blending ability) of paint, and the increased depth of color would serve no useful purpose here.

Figure 48 A paint layer was applied with the knife to deprive the surface of some of its tooth. Next, the smooth surface left by the knife was gone over with the soft-hair blender, leaving grooves which will hold the next paint layer. For this operation, it is best to move the blender in parallel strokes. Should several underpaintings be planned, a stronger tooth will be necessary and a bristle brush can be used. The exceedingly rough texture produced in this manner can be made smoother with the soft hair blender, if needed.

(3) Impasto painting should never be carried out on a toothless surface.

### UNDERPAINTING IN STAGES

If a canvas surface is too smooth to support the subsequent layer of paint, it should be provided with new tooth. This is done as demonstrated in Fig. 48.

Because several thin applications will dry more quickly than one heavy layer of paint, it is always preferable to avoid *one heavy impasto,* for the superimposed underpaintings must be done on a dry surface. Under normal conditions, an impasto 1/16″ thick will dry in about three days, provided quick drying colors are used. Hence, whatever color is chosen for underpainting, some umber should be added to it in order to accelerate its drying.

Siccative should not be used to accelerate the drying process because, as mentioned before, it acts well only in thin applications. When siccative is added to a thick layer of paint, *the rapidly forming tough skin on its surface will materially delay the drying of paint underneath this skin.* Within about ten days, three underpaintings in moderate impasto can be done, and any desirable texture produced.

To pause for a moment—I have advocated a good number of impasti and explained their merit. But more often than not, *one* underpainting will suffice.

It would appear, also, that all kinds of textures should be treated in the same manner. This, of course, is not necessarily so. First, a thick paint layer need not be rough; its surface can be perfectly smooth. Then, the smooth underpainting, as well as the roughly brushed passages can be used for subsequent glazing, which would produce entirely different effects in each instance.

Hence, we have textures appearing in the following configurations:

1 Surface roughness achieved by various means, prepared for a final impasto which can have various surface characteristics depending on what kind of brush or knife will be used to produce it.

2 Similar rough underpaintings used for eventual glazes.

3 Perfectly smooth-surfaced underpainting with a final glaze or a smooth, thin, opaque surface.

4 A smooth underpainting that will never be covered by an overpaint, but will remain in its orignal color and serve as part of the final effect.

## SIX BASIC RECOMMENDATIONS

Here are six points to bear in mind:

1 Underpainting in a single application should be done with the painting knife on a canvas with sufficient tooth. If a brush is used (for details, etc.), its marks should be smoothed with the painting knife, because the texture left by the brush will interfere with the final texture of the painting—unless a very heavy impasto is used to cover it up.

2 If tooth is lacking, the smooth surface produced by the knife should be slightly grooved with a soft-hair blender.

3 If an extra rough texture is desired, the underpainting (or a few underpaintings) can be carried out with bristle brushes.

4 If glazes are to be used, the underpainting should be especially prepared for the occasion, as I will explain in a moment.

5 Undesired roughness of the underpainting should be sanded. The best material for this purpose is a fine carborundum paper.

6 *Paint used in underpainting should be as stiff as possible; it should not be diluted with the medium.* If it is too stiff to be moved easily with the brush, a little Copal Painting Medium should be added.

## GENERAL OBSERVATIONS

As I have suggested, the purpose of underpainting is to enrich the coloristic appearance of a painting and to create an interesting variety of textures. Underpainting also serves to stimulate the painter's color sense and to give him a first taste of the coloristic and compositional problems involved in the painting.

In principle, this type of painting does not represent a radical departure from the alla prima method, for it is based on analogous principles. Underpainting is worked out with the same intrinsic logic; yet it is a more complex technique, allowing greater elaborations and a wider scope. While you underpaint—that is, when you work in stages—your pictorial ideas can mature slowly, and you can summon up greater technical resources.

At this point, you may wonder why you could not paint final colors directly on the white canvas. This would be the case only when you work alla prima. Besides, a white surface does not contribute to the coloristic appearance of a painting. But it is only on the rarest occasions that a painter finishes his work by employing only one layer of paint on a canvas. In reality, his second corrective application of paint actually constitutes painting on an underpainting. He does not *call* it an "underpainting" simply because his first layer is usually just an unsuccessful painting that has to be covered up.

In the history of art, only the Impressionists began painting with the final colors on white canvas ground. But very few did not overpaint the initial sketch; that is, few Impressionists worked alla prima. One of these few was Van Gogh; his initial heavy impasti were not covered up. Cézanne's late work is all alla prima on white canvas; frequently the white canvas (untouched by paint) remains in evidence in many small (and even large) areas of the painting. It should be noted, however, that the alla prima work of these painters has nothing in common with the classic alla prima method.

## A BRIEF HISTORY OF CLASSIC TECHNIQUES

The perfect technique of the Van Eyck School (early in the 15th century) has never been surpassed—seldom even duplicated. The painting of these early Flemish masters carry as many as four underpaintings in some places. These layers were built up with colors of a much lower key than are seen in the final painting. Contrary to previously held opinion, tempera underpainting was not used by these masters.

Some years ago, in the Laboratory of the Royal Museum in Brussels, I had the opportunity to examine under a microscope a particle of the cross section of paint (including the gesso ground) from Van Eyck's *Adoration of the Lamb*. From microscopic and microchemical analyses of the samples, it was possible to make definite deductions as to the technique of these paintings.

The greatest Flemish masters of the late 15th to 17th centuries—Bosch, Brueghel, Rubens— painted alla prima in the identical manner that I have described earlier. Ruben's large paintings were partly underpainted in lighter colors. The Italians of the 16th and 17th centuries (Tintoretto and Titian), as well as the Dutch painters (Rembrandt, Frans Hals), and El Greco—all painted on dark grounds. Areas that received transparent color applications (not frequently seen in these paintings) were underpainted in colors appropriate to the glazes that followed.

Eighteenth century masters, like Tiepolo and Guardi, worked on light, pastel-colored grounds; the color of these grounds (or underpaintings) generally contrasted with the final colors. Goya (late 18th to early 19th century) largely followed the precepts of the old masters, mainly those of Rubens, and so did Delacroix. The Barbizon painters (mid-19th century) faintly echoed earlier methods; but the Impressionists radically departed from them. By that time (last quarter of the 19th century), these methods had gone largely into oblivion, only to be revived about fifty years later.

## COLOR IN UNDERPAINTING

In underpainting, two characteristics of paint should be considered: its body and its color. If the paint has body, it means that it is dense and therefore opaque. Thus a pigment that requires a considerable quantity of the vehicle

(linseed oil) to be converted into paint will not possess enough body to serve in underpainting; it will, as a rule, be a glazing color. However, when mixed with a *body color* (like white), even a glazing color can be used in underpainting.

Flake white, the densest and most solid of our paints, will be our most important underpainting color. As I have mentioned, it is compounded with only 10% oil, whereas Prussian blue, for example, may require 100% of the binder. Hence, to reduce the amount of oil in the underpainting, flake white will enter into mixtures with every color. In landscape painting, I cannot think of any color that would be used unmixed in underpainting.

An important coloristic principle which should guide us is this: superimposed colors should contrast with one another. The term, *contrast,* covers a wide range: from the strongest contrast that complementary colors would provide (green and red or blue and orange) to much closer color approximations. Such superimposed contrasting colors, when judiciously exploited, yield the strongest coloristic effects, whereas the superimposition of identical colors would serve no coloristic purpose.

What advantages do we gain when we underpaint in colors that are complementary or will contrast with the overpainting? Optically and psychologically, such contrasts offer us a challenge. We know that contrast between colors increases their mutual activity; on the other hand, the more closely two colors are related, the weaker the effect; should we use *identical* colors, one on top of another, we would not be able to see what we are doing. Thus, when painting red on red, for example, our gain would be nil. But if the red color is superimposed on green, our capacity to feel the red is immensely intensified.

## COLOR MIXTURES USED IN UNDERPAINTING

Here are some basic mixtures:

*Blue tones:* white and any one of our blue colors—ultramarine, Prussian, phthalo.

*Blue-green tones:* any one of the blues, white,

and either viridian green or phthalo green; also white, Prussian blue, and ochre.

*Yellow-green tones:* white, Hansa yellow, and one of our blue or one of our green colors.

*Pale yellow tones:* white and ochre. *Strong yellow tones:* white and Hansa or cadmium yellow.

*Pink tones:* white and Venetian or cadmium red, or burnt siena.

*Gray tones:* white and umber; or white, umber, and Prussian blue.

These are all the colors that would enter into the underpainting of landscapes of any kind.

# CHAPTER 11

# Skies, trees, rocks, water

First, a brief review of some general principles of oil painting technique.

As a rule, the underpainting should be a *light tonality;* dark tones will not provide the effect of luminosity. A dark underpainting, however, is useful for *scumbling.*

A general rule for painting wet-in-wet is that *light colors (or tones) should be painted into dark colors.* This practice contrasts with watercolor painting, where dark accents are always applied to the white surface of the paper. The reason for this difference is simple: in oil painting, a light color passage will invariably contain white. When a dark color is painted into one containing white, muddiness frequently results. However, this does not imply that such procedure is always taboo.

*The more thoroughly two or more colors are mixed, the duller they become* because the color matter is more evenly dispersed. The mixing of paint should be done very slightly, especially when you use a painting knife. In many cases, the colors taken up by the knife can be mixed directly on the canvas. Two or three colors swept onto the canvas with the knife, *without mixing,* can produce extraordinary coloristic effects. One should remember, however, that passages in a dull color also have their place in the general scheme of a painting.

To repeat: the surface should be oiled with the medium before you paint. All paints should be conditioned with Copal Concentrate to improve their working quality.

In the following pages, I shall demonstrate the painting of all elements that go into the representation of landscapes.

### SKIES

For underpainting, use one of the following, mixed with white: ochre, Hansa yellow, Venetion red, cadmium red, burnt siena.

Overpainting in predominantly blue semitransparent colors over such an underpainting would produce a variety of effects: lesser or greater radiance, depending on the strength of the underlying yellow color; and lesser or stronger luminosity, depending on the activity of the pink underpainting. Thus, a pink produced from cadmium red and white, for example, will be much more active than one mixed from burnt siena and white. Of course, the overpaints must be applied thinly, to allow the color of the underpainting to assert itself.

Should you wish to scumble on the sky area and thus make it semi-opaque, a gray color mixed from white, umber, and Prussian blue can be used. Where transparency is not required, this combination of colors is best for a gray underpainting because it is neutral, and also fast drying. If the underpainting is sufficiently dark, a lighter tone of contrasting color can be scumbled on top of it.

For example: underpaint in red (any one of our red colors) with some white and umber added. (This addition of about one third white will not materially influence a strong iron oxide red.) On top of it, scumble a gray, or a pink, or a yellowish color.

In the color chart, Fig. 49, a few treatments of the sky area are demonstrated.

In painting a clear blue sky, any one of the suggested underpaintings can be chosen, and any one of the blues. Starting with a darker shade of blue at the top, the color should be made progressively lighter by the addition of white. In the lower parts, some Naples yellow may be added. Such is the "normal" appearance of a blue sky: always a darker blue at the top; at the distant horizon line, the blue may entirely disappear. The only objection to a sky treated in this manner is that it may easily appear like a picture postcard.

In the initial application of the sky area, the treatment of textures should be considered. Clouds appear to be palpable, compared to the void of a blue sky. Hence, it is reasonable to treat the sky smoothly, and to limit any slight impasto to the cloud formations. Smooth surfaces can be produced best by means of the knife which we use for blending colors and also for painting large surfaces. If a bristle brush is used, its harsh demarcations can be flattened with our soft-hair blender. For delicate blending of colors, especially in the cloud area, this brush is indispensable. For painting clouds, the large, round sable brush is most useful.

## PAINTING TREES

Occasionally, I hear my students asking how to paint a cottonwood, a eucalyptus, a willow tree, etc. Always bearing in mind the student's understanding of esthetic principles, my invariable answer is that the painter should not be concerned with the illustrative aspect of the painting. The particular identification of a species, although it does have illustrative value, is of no account, artistically. Our chief concern is limited to the general representation of the textures of foliage, recognized as textures rather than particular species of trees. And the principal difference regarding texture will be between deciduous and coniferous trees.

We cannot always say with certainty which kind of underpainting is best. For underpainting trees, however, as well as all verdant matter, yellow is not only the best color but the only one I would choose. The reason? If overpainted thinly, yellow, glowing from within, will impart life to the superimposed color. No other color is as effective coming from within a glaze, or through a semi-opaque color application.

Now you may ask, what if I plan to paint trees entirely in opaque color? First, this cannot be previsualized with absolute certainty. Second, if the overpaint is opaque the yellow underpainting will just be there to serve as an underpainting for shape and texture, without being utilized coloristically.

What kind of yellow should be used? This depends entirely on the space occupied by the particular tree, clump of trees, or a forest. The closer the trees are to the viewer, the stronger the color should be. Thus, we may start with Hansa yellow and white in the foreground, then change to ochre and white as we move into the background.

To remind the reader, I recommend Hansa yellow instead of cadmium yellow for underpainting because the strong aniline dye of the Hansa will color the white to a high-keyed yellow. Besides, it is much more useful for this purpose than the oil-rich, slow-drying cadmium. When the tree area is in the far distance, and too small to be treated as a separate unit, it will receive a color similar to the general color scheme used for that location.

49A

49B

49C

Figure 49A  The underpainting was light yellow (Hansa yellow and white). For the overpainting, a blue prepared from Prussian blue, umber, and white was used. In 49B, the light pink underpainting was overpainted with phthalo blue and white. Examples 49C and 49D, represent the effects of scumbling. In both instances, the underpainting was dull gray— umber, Prussian blue, and white —the quick drying combination. Here the underlying color was unimportant, for it eventually disappears under the subsequent paint layer. In 49C, the paint layer was bluish green: ultramarine, viridian green, and white. Into this wet surface, applied with the knife, white clouds were also scumbled with the knife, and then blended with the soft hair blender. In 49D, the color was mixed from Prussian blue, umber, Venetian red, and white; the cloud effect was produced with the knife, using Naples yellow and white. In Figures 49E and 49F, transparencies are seen again; these are due to the underpainting of light yellow, mixed from ochre and white. In 49E, ultramarine, umber, and white were used thinly enough to make the yellowish color impart luminosity to the overpaint. The fleecy clouds

49D

were scumbled into the wet paint with a large, round sable brush; finally, the soft transitions were obtained by brushing the paint with the soft hair blender. To produce such effects successfully, a considerable viscosity of paint is necessary. As we know, such viscosity can easily be brought about by using larger than usual admixtures of Copal Concentrate. To make the white paint more liquid—an essential quality in scumbling—it should be thinned with a sufficient amount of Copal Painting Medium Heavy in addition to the concentrate. The last example, 49F, received a thin overpaint of ultramarine, viridian green, and white (approximating the color of cerulean blue); the billowing clouds were painted with a large, round sable brush. In the shadow parts, ultramarine, burnt siena, and white were used; white rendered the lightest effects. Here, too, the colors were generously conditioned with the concentrate. Perhaps it bears repeating: when working on a wet paint layer, our intention is to paint *on it*, not to sweep the underlying paint aside with the brush that moves over its surface. A sufficiently viscous paint will not be easily agitated by the soft hair of the sable brush, or by the knife.

49E

49F

50A 50B

50C 50D

50E 50F

Figure 50 This represents a range of greens. 50A Cadmium yellow medium and Prussian blue. 50B The same colors with white. 50C Umber and cadmium yellow light. 50D The same colors with white. 50E Viridian green and cadmium yellow. 50F The same colors with white.

50G

50H

50I

50J

50K

50L

50G Viridian green, Naples yellow, ultramine blue. 50H The same colors with white. 50I Ultramarine blue and Naples yellow. 50J A glaze of Prussian blue and burnt siena on a yellow underpainting. 50K Black and cadmium yellow. 50L The same colors with white.

**Figure 51A** Underpainting. Sky: pink (Venetian red and white). Foliage: yellow (Hansa yellow and white). Ground and tree trunk: ochre, umber, and white.

**Figure 51B** Over the entire area of the foliage, a glaze of Prussian blue and burnt siena was applied.

**Figure 51C** Into this glaze, an impasto mixed from cadmium yellow and white was scumbled in broad strokes with a bristle brush.

**Figure 51D** Branches were added, using umber and Prussian blue. Tree trunk: umber, Prussian blue, white. Foreground: umber, cadmium yellow, Prussian blue. Sky: Prussian blue, umber, and white.

In the overpainting, the greens of trees seen in full light will vary from the strongest yellow-green to pale blue-green. The latter will always appear in the remote distance. The highest-keyed green color, as we know, will be produced with cadmium yellow medium or dark, mixed with any one of our blues. White will cut the intensity of these colors, which, as a rule, will rarely be used full strength. Milder greens can be obtained from viridian green and one of the yellows: cadmium light, strontium, or zinc. When Naples yellow, ultramarine, and viridian green are used, the trees will appear locked in the most distant planes. For coniferous trees, cadmium yellow and Prussian blue can be used, with or without white or black, depending on the occasion.

Enumerating these colors alone serves the theory well; but the fact is that that too much, or too little, of one color or another may upset the entire scheme. And how can one explain the quantitative relations of colors—any colors—by means of words. Hence, the following color chart (Fig. 50), containing different color mixtures, may help to illuminate our problems.

### PAINTING TREES: DEMONSTRATION 1

The underpainting in Fig. 51A shows one striking feature: the borderlines of the tree appear thoroughly blurred. That is, the transitions between the sky and the area of the foliage, the ground, and so forth, are so well blended that it is impossible to say where the contours of the object are to be found. Depending on the particular occasion, blending can be done with a brush or knife, whichever appears more practical. However, the final operation should be done with the knife, to do away with the harsh demarcations left by the bristles of the brush.

In Fig. 51B, this advantage of blending contours in the underpainting becomes explicit. A glaze of Prussian blue and burnt siena was spread over the entire surface that would, more or less, be occupied by the mass of foliage. This area meets the preliminary yellow color of the sky in a soft transition. Nothing is easier than to make this transition evanescent.

Why have we applied the dark glaze first? Because we plan to use it for the shadows that gather in the recessions between the branches. Is a glaze the best application for the darkest

**Figure 53** *The Wilderness* (26″ x 44″). The technique here differs from the preceding painting in one respect. The ground area, in contrast to the rest of the painting (which is treated in impasto), is covered entirely by a thin, translucent glaze. Here, an ochre and white underpainting was glazed with viridian green and strontium yellow; some Prussian blue and burnt siena were used for the darker definitions.

part of the foliage? Yes, it will have the greatest depth, and will correspond to the textural impression that the foliage gives us: its palpable appearance when seen in full light, and the veil-like dematerialization of the shadowy parts. When proceeding in this manner, there is no need to *paint the shadows;* you can give your attention exclusively to the branches that capture the light.

These branches were treated with impasto, using cadmium yellow and white. In this instance, a bristle brush was used.

In Fig. 51C, the strong impasto brushed on top of the glaze acquired some of the glaze's blue color and, in the process, the yellow turned light green here and there. I said that using the glaze for the shadow part is best. This belief does not preclude the possibility of painting the shadows opaquely. But, in this case, both the texture of the light and the dark parts would become uniform, hence they would lack variability.

In Fig. 51D, the following steps were taken. The sky was painted around the tree and with-

in it, here and there, to admit some light through the mass of the foliage. At this point, I should make it clear that this is not the standard procedure in classic technique where you would paint the background first (in this case, the sky), and superimpose the object on it. But here, the simplicity of the motif allowed the use of a divergent method; besides, we should never be bound by strict orthodoxy.

Next, the branches and tree trunk were sketched. For the branches, our darkest color was chosen: burnt siena and Prussian blue. The tree trunk was painted with the knife, using umber and white; the same treatment was accorded the ground area, with the addition of cadmium yellow.

All the fine demarcations were produced with the scriptliner, and (besides white) only four colors were used: Prussian blue, umber, burnt siena, cadmium yellow.

### PAINTING TREES: DEMONSTRATION 2

I mentioned that we are not concerned here

**Figure 54** *The Forest* (22″ x 26″). The tree trunk in the front received three consecutive underpaintings; two of these were produced with bristle brushes and the last one with the knife, which pressed the paint material into the heavy texture, and made the top surface appear relatively smooth. At this point, no details were painted on the surface. These details were executed into a thin semi-glaze which did not fight the dark delineations marking the trunk texture. The colors used were our old standbys: Prussian blue, umber, and white; these were mixed to a silvery gray tonality. Practically every tree was painted from a pen and ink study, made from nature. As in Fig 56, the entire area of the forest in the background was first glazed with Prussian blue and burnt siena over an underpainting of ochre, some umber, and white. Dark and light details were painted into this unifying tone. The surface occupied by the pine branches was underpainted in a much brighter yellow (ochre and white) which gave this particular motif greater luminosity than the motifs in the background. In this example, the importance of painting the sky first is well demonstrated: the outer contours of all the elements of the composition are so ragged that to paint the sky around them would not be feasible. Hence, the sky was painted first in its principal color and then sky tones were well blended with the yellow area underlying the foliage of the trees. This yellow, in a halo-like effect, remains visible around the fringes of the foliage.

with a particular kind of tree, but rather with the character of its skeletal structure and the texture of its foliage. Depending on the tools—bristle brushes, sable brushes, or knives, and how they are used—different textures can be produced. In the preceding example, a bristle brush was chosen.

In the demonstration in Fig. 52, I have worked with the scriptliner alone, to suggest two different coniferous trees. The procedure in painting both examples, as well as in the underpainting, was the same as in Fig. 51. First, a dark glaze was made to cover the entire area of the trees; then the differentiated foliage was painted with impasto, using cadmium yellow, viridian green, and white.

Tree studies by the author are also seen in Fig. 54, *The Forest* (20″ x 26″); Fig. 53, *Wilderness* (26″ x 44″); and Fig. 55, *The Poet* (16″ x 20″). Every one of the trees in these paintings had its origin in a drawing made in Northwestern Canada. In fact, hundreds of exact tree studies were made right on location, for it is very important that to be authentic the land-scape painter should familiarize himself with the anatomy of things, both botanic and arboreal.

### PAINTING A FOREST

In Fig. 56, the painting of a forest is demonstrated. Before referring to the technique, let us theorize about the problem at hand. We could paint a forest and compose it from so many well defined trees. When the forest area is large, we could conceivably paint a hundred or several hundred individual trees. Would such an undertaking be foolish? Not necessarily. Conceptions of this kind existed in some ancient school of painting; I am thinking here particularly of the Flemish and German masters and their passion for minutiae. Presumably, some painters could be able, even today, to manage such a detailed style of painting—at least we may theoretically suppose this. However, there is a healthier and more practical method of dealing with such problems.

In this shorthand method, the expanse of the forest will be treated as one shadowy mass and

▼Figure 55A *The Poet* (16″ x 20″). The tree shows the entire gamut of technical devices that can be used in oil painting. To begin with the underpainting: sky, light pink; crown of the tree, ochre and white; trunk, light gray (Prussian blue, umber, and white); background, light gray; foreground, ochre and white. The second step was oiling the canvas and applying glazes: umber, on the center and trunk of the tree; a glaze of cadmium yellow over the area of the foliage; and a glaze of Prussian blue and umber in the foreground. The third step was the actual painting. Sky: ultramarine blue, umber, Naples yellow. Dark accents of the area of the tree: umber and Prussian blue. Light accents: cadmium yellow and white. Dead branches on the right side: white, grayed with umber. Background: Naples yellow scumbled over the gray ground; raw siena and viridian green for the green effects; ultramarine, white, and black for the area of the lakes. All definitions of the distant trees and other linear marks were painted with Prussian blue and umber. The chief instruments used were: scriptliner, striper, and palette knife. (Because, in this painting, so much emphasis is put on the variability of texture, a reproduction, no matter how accurate, cannot adequately convey the impression of the original.)

Figure 55B   Detail of the upper branches. ▶

Figure 55C   Detail showing brushstrokes. ▶

55A

Figure 56 The entire expanse of the forest was covered with a thin glaze of Prussian blue and burnt siena on a dull yellowish underpainting (ochre, a little umber, and white). Next, the few definitions of trees were drawn with a scriptliner into the shadowy area, using burnt siena and Prussian blue. Here the color was concentrated; therefore it appears black. Finally, here and there a tree appears in full light because it is placed in the forefront; hence, it is not overshadowed by other trees.

Figure 57 The technique shown in this example can be used best where the areas of shadows are sufficiently large, for only such large areas can be glazed. First, a solid underlayer of paint must be provided for the entire surface. The last underpainting (or the first, if a fine-grained fabric is used) should be light, and should show variations consistent with the character of the rock. In other words, the rock should be modeled in light colors only because these will be—more or less—the final colors. The dark glazes are used for shadows and to indicate the rock's irregular surface. ▶

only a few trees will be differentiated: these will catch light, hence they will materialize clearly in their particular shape. In this example, there is no doubt whatever that we are facing a vast, densely wooded section, yet only a few single trees are actually articulated.

### PAINTING ROCKS: DEMONSTRATION 1

To represent stone masses, four principal techniques can be used: (1) glazing on a smooth, solid substratum of paint (Fig. 57); (2) painting in rough impasto first, and then glazing (Fig. 58); (3) painting in impasto, using a brush (Fig. 59); and (4) using a knife (Fig. 60).

In the method exemplified in Fig. 57, the entire surface of the rock should receive one or more underpaintings to make the tooth of the fabric disappear completely under the layer of paint. In our example, executed on a very fine fabric, one layer of paint provided a marked impasto. The surface of this impasto should be perfectly smooth. The knife which we called a blender is best suited to produce such a surface.

Why should the surface of this impasto underpainting be smooth? Because this "underpainting" will serve as our *final* painting; the parts of the rock seen in full light will not have to be altered in color and texture. Only the design of its stratification and the parts in shade will be glazed.

This can be done in the following manner. The entire surface can receive a light glaze, which we call a middle tone because it is neither light nor dark. Into this middle tone, the shadows and linear definitions of the rock strata are painted with a darker color. For those parts of the rock seen in full light, wipe off the initial glaze with a cheesecloth. In other words, the glaze is eliminated wherever required, thus uncovering the original underpainting. Now you might ask: why not leave these areas in their original condition without the initial glaze? This too can be done in instances when the areas of shade are insignificant.

As to colors, the following were used for the underpainting (in this example, the final color of the rock was unobstructed by shadows, and unmarked by stratifications): white slightly mixed with ochre, for yellowish tints; and white with a minimal admixture of Mars black, for gray tints. Together, these tints produce dull light greenish tones. For the glaze, umber and Prussian blue were used. Depending on the density of the glaze, and the relative preponderance of umber or Prussian blue, one can produce light brownish or bluish tones to the deepest black. For broad definition of the glazed areas, a round sable brush was used; for the fine delineaments, a scriptliner.

### PAINTING ROCKS: DEMONSTRATION 2

Fig. 58 illustrates the use of impasti and glazes. They were carried out as follows. The mass of the rock was divided into two areas: one to receive light, the other to remain in shade. The first area was painted in a dark bluish gray mixed from umber, Prussian blue, and white. This color was *stippled* on (*dabbed* rather than brushed) in the following manner: paint of heavy consistency was spread over the area with a bristle brush. Then, the paint surface was made still rougher by pressing the flat side of the blending knife up and down over it. Such an operation creates a heavy, stippled texture in the mass of paint. Finally, with the soft-hair blender, the ridges and hillocks of the agitated paint surface were slightly flattened, and allowed to dry thoroughly. Thus, we have created a rather dark, richly textured surface on the light side of the rock.

The side in shade was treated with a smooth impasto in a light color, just as in Fig. 57. Now, it should be remembered that the activity of a glazed surface depends on both the light tone and the color of the underpainting. *A light yellow underpainting will make a superimposed glaze much more active than a light gray underpainting.*

The next step was to apply the glaze over the entire surface: the smooth passage as well as the one in rough impasto. Again, this dark glaze was prepared from umber and Prussian blue (burnt siena could also have been used with Prussian blue). Next, with the edge of the painting knife, a mixture of ochre and white was applied over the rough surface. This light paint, carried by the straight edge of the knife, attached itself only to the top surface of the rock. In the crevices, the dark glaze remained untouched, thus suggesting the appearance of a rough rock surface in full light. Next, on the side of the *shade*, the glaze was modified by thinning it (that is wiping) with cheesecloth in places, and by making it appear darker in spots by using a denser color. Again, a scriptliner and a striper were used for linear definition.

On several occasions, I have suggested using Prussian blue and umber or burnt siena for shadows. One might ask, are there any other workable combinations? As long as you are dealing with natural appearances, the reasons for this choice are logical: a shadow seen out-of-doors (and often indoors) is bluish; so we shall have to use a mixture of colors that contains blue, and another color to modify it. Hence, any one of our blues could be used with any one of our brown colors. However, I prefer the aforementioned three colors, which does not necessarily qualify them as being the best for everyone concerned.

### PAINTING ROCKS: DEMONSTRATION 3

Our third demonstration is presented in Fig. 59. This rock formation was finished entirely with bristle brushes and the striper, but the two underpaintings were done with the knife, providing a solid surface. Therefore the choice of colors was dictated by one consideration only: quick drying. Consequently, umber and white were used. Why was a brush not used for the second underpainting? Simply, because its texture would interfere with the final paint texture. It should be kept in mind that chaotic, contradictory impasti, one piled on top of another, are rarely attractive to the eye.

The colors of the top layer of paint were: chrome oxide green opaque, burnt siena, black, and white. And the strategy of this choice rested on the following consideration: burnt siena and white provide a dull pink which is pleasant to use in combination with the dull green. Black, white, and burnt siena yield a warm, reddish gray; all these colors are eminently suited for painting rather low-keyed masses of rock.

### PAINTING ROCKS: DEMONSTRATION 4

Our fourth example, Fig. 60, was finished with the painting knife, covering an underpainting that left some of the original tooth of the canvas in evidence. The knife, as we have seen, can be used for all kinds of applications, ranging from the thinnest glazes to the heaviest impasti. In the example under discussion, only one layer of opaque paint was meant to achieve the final effect. This top layer, after drying, would not have produced a satisfactory surface to paint upon unless it was sandpapered (the particular texture of the knife work does not lend itself to overpaints).

Working with the knife offers great advantages. A quantity of paint—several colors at one time—can be taken on the blade and swept with abandon onto the canvas. When working in this manner, you can produce extraordinary effects. Accidental effects—not really calculated—may appear, often belying the fact that you may be just a beginner. Often an unsatisfactory initial passage can be radically altered by spreading on it another, and still another layer of paint. Of course, such an operation requires a perfect instrument. Then again, if the effects produced by the knife fail to satisfy you, scrape it all off. Starting afresh, again and again, you can in the end become unexpectedly successful.

Besides these four rock studies, four paintings with rocks as their main themes are seen in Figs. 61, 62, 63, and 64.

### ROCK COLORS

The colors mentioned for painting rocks were: black, ochre, burnt siena, umber, Prussian blue, and chrome oxide green dull, in addition to white. Of course, not more than three of these colors should be chosen at one time, for larger mixtures would indicate the painter's confusion rather than his purposefulness. Moreover, complex mixtures could hardly be remembered and repeated when needed. These colors are of the dull variety—when *normally* intermixed. As we know, even dull colors, when taken up unmixed on a knife and then applied with one or two strokes, will produce exciting effects.

Can brilliant colors also be used for rocks?

**Figure 59** The rocks were painted with a bristle brush and a flat sable brush in a relatively smooth impasto in opaque colors, using white as well as ochre, burnt siena, ultramarine, and black (in other words, pale yellow, pink, and gray tones). The dark shades are mixed from ochre and black, which yields green, and from burnt siena and black, which gives dark brown.▶

**Figure 58** This example shows a different technique, inasmuch as the part which received the light was underpainted in dark colors and in rough impasto, whereas the one in shade was underpainted very smoothly in light colors. Hence the underpainting, 58A, looks like a negative of the original. In the overpainting, 58B, I spread a dark glaze (Prussian blue and umber) over the light, as well as the dark, surface. Next, I applied thick, very light paint with a knife to the part in light. Because it is spread with the knife, this paint can reach only the top of the impasto, and the dark glaze which remains in the crevices cannot be affected by it. Hence, the dark glaze will suggest the crevices in the rock's surface. Finally, the initial glaze in the shadow part was strengthened, or made lighter in spots, and embroidered, as it were, with marks indicating the rock's stratification.▼

◄ Figure 60  A painting of rocks, mainly executed with a painting knife, plus a scriptliner for linear definitions.

Figure 61  *The Burning Bush* (38″ x 48″). The fantastically eroded sandstone dominates the picture. In the vast expanse of the background, rocky peaks move restlessly like windswept ripples in an immense body of water. Together, the peaks form a curtain that heightens the weird effect of the *dramatis personae* in the foreground. In every respect— shape, color, texture—this central motif differs from the rest of the rocky landscape. All of the background shows heavy impasti, especially where the peaks are heightened by a strong, white, linear pattern. The colors used in the background, besides white, were: Mars brown, viridian green, and raw siena. The sky was the only area painted with the knife. Here, as you can clearly see in the reproduction, a light color (Naples yellow and white) was scumbled into a dark blue-green mixed from Prussian blue, umber, Naples yellow, and white. The sandstone and the ground around its lower part were underpainted in Mars yellow and white, and glazed with viridian green, Prussian blue, and umber. Highlights on this area were painted with Naples yellow and white, and those on trees in the foreground, with cadmium yellow. The burning bush, seen in the opening of the rock on the right side, shows glints of cadmium orange. There can be no mistake about it; this detail was put in for no other purpose than to justify the portentous title of the picture.

Figure 62 *Three Lakes* (36" x 40"). The vast mountain fastness is a free interpretation of a region in Northwestern Canada. With the exception of the soft, light meadow in the center—as well as the smaller details, and the linear definition—the entire picture was done with the painting knife. Sky: white, strontium yellow, black. Mountains: viridian green, Prussian blue, raw siena, white. Ground—top level: ochre, white, some umber. Lower levels: zinc yellow, dark ochre, umber, Prussian blue, white. Water: Prussian blue, viridian green, ochre, white. Dark accents were painted with umber and Prussian blue. It is important to note that when several colors are mentioned as having been used on one area, this does not imply that all three or four hues were mixed together throughout the entire surface. The combination varies from spot to spot, and the quantity of one color or another differs also; hence the gradation and variations of even two colors can be quite large.

**Figure 63** *The Moon and the Rock* (26″ x 40″). This painting differs from those in preceding examples because here the rock masses were finished almost entirely in glazes applied with the painting knife. Such effects are frequently seen in our examples, but to make them work on a large surface is quite difficult. And the difficulty is twofold: it concerns texture, as well as color. Our main concern is to make a dramatic showing. Therefore, colors of the glaze and the surrounding area must be chosen carefully to avoid monotony of such a large body. As to the glaze, it was applied to a surface carrying three layers of paint. Because of the rough texture of the fabric, the underpaintings—all done with the knife—formed an interesting textural pattern. Their colors differed: the motifs in the background were light gray; those in the foreground were warmer, of a yellowish tonality. The color of the glaze was mixed from ultramarine, burnt siena, and, in places, raw siena. The whole structure was set off by the dramatic color of the sky; here, cadmium orange and white were modified by a small addition of ochre. We should note that when ochre is placed next to cadmium red (or orange), its color value appears green. In this situation, it is complementary to red; hence ochre is capable of neutralizing red —that is, lowering its hue—without altering its intrinsic color value.

Depending on the nature of a composition, even a high-keyed color can be chosen, especially when the need arises to differentiate between distant rocks and those nearby. In such a case, rocks in the foreground may be a strong red color, for example: Venetian red, cadmium red, or Mars violet in intermixtures, modified, here and there, by umber, black, and white. Considering the strength of these red colors, Mars black would be a logical choice to cope with them.

Then we may ask: when is a rock a mere rock? When its mass does not exceed a certain size. When the rocky mass occupies a large area, we shall think of them as mountains, rocky mountains in this case. These, even in the distance, need not be pale blue. They may be painted a brilliant, strong blue (such as one sees on some landscapes by the Flemish master, Joachim Patinir), or even in a brilliant red, should some special occasion call for the use of such colors. In short, the painter should not necessarily be guided by considerations of being "true to nature," for paintings have their own intrinsic truth, which often is at odds with the ostensible image of objects seen in nature.

### PAINTING WATER

When I speak of water, I refer to any conceivable situation except conventional seascapes with dramatic splashing of waves and surf. To digress for a moment, we may ask who among the great masters painted thundering seascapes or the snowy peaks above the timber line? No one did. Consequently we must conclude that the colossal, the super grandiose in nature does not lend itself very well to pictorial treatment. By the same token, some common weeds have more pictorial allure than the most gorgeous orchid or chrysanthemum. In short, what is great in nature may not be great as a subject for a picture.

To return to my discussion of water in any conceivable form—lake, mountain stream, puddle and so forth—how are we going to underpaint it? Bodies of water seem to look "wetter" when they are scumbled rather than glazed. To

**Figure 64A** *After Sunset* (16" x 20"). This demonstration serves to point out certain effects seen in the work of early Flemish painters. In fact, these effects first suggested to me that a hard resin medium must have been used by the early masters; the conjecture is justified if we consider the virtual imperishability of these paintings. Specifically, the high, "soupy" impasto used, especially in the greens, points to the use of a resinous medium. These impasti seem to endow the plants, grasses, tree foliage, and so forth, with a strange vitality. In Figures 64B and 64C, all the trees in the foreground can be seen to carry impasti that are in strong contrast to the rest of the surface, where the paint is entirely smooth. The underpainting proceeded step-by-step as follows.

Sky: pink. Ground: dull, yellowish gray. Rock: ochre, white, umber. Now the overpainting. Sky: a glaze of viridian green, ultramarine, umber, and white, applied very thinly with the knife (we have the impression of the pink color coming from within). Rock: glazes of viridian green and burnt siena for the darks, and Mars yellow for the lights; scumbles of ochre and white for the highlights. The background was glazed with viridian green, white, and a little umber to dull the color. The trees in the foreground were painted with burnt siena, Prussian blue, and cadmium yellow; in the background, with viridian green.

**Figure 64B** Detail of lower left hand corner.

**Figure 64C** Detail of brushstrokes.

elaborate on scumbling first: a neutral gray, a bluish or greenish gray, is all that we would like to use for underpainting. Why? Experience teaches us that other colors—yellowish or pink tonalities, for example—are impractical. This is not necessarily because they run counter to the feeling we associate with water; but when such tonalities are used in final painting, they will have to be completely opaque, hence they cannot be scumbled. To sum up: a gray underpainting seems to be most useful for whatever color we may choose as the final one, in painting water.

In Fig. 65A, the light effects were produced by means of a scriptliner on a solid layer of paint, mixed from ochre, black, Prussian blue, and white. In Fig. 65B, water was painted with the palette knife using the following colors opaquely: Prussian blue, viridian green, ochre, and black (in addition to white)—four colors in this case. But remembering my previous observation, you could say that four colors are too many to be conveniently remembered. However, we may not consider black and white

to be "true" colors, since they rather represent lack of color.

In Fig. 66A, a very simple process is seen. Here the underpainting—using our old stand-bys, Prussian blue, umber, and white—is a light, bluish slate-gray. At the upper edge (presumably the distant shore), a glaze of Prussian blue, viridian green, and black (some white was added which helped reduce its transparency) was spread evenly with a bristle brush and then rubbed in with the side of the hand, in a manner similar to rubbing varnish into the paint surface. The delicate blending of the glaze was done with cheesecloth. The rest of the surface shows the underpainting, which remains unchanged.

In the last example, Fig. 66B, the underpainting was again a light bluish gray. This disappeared entirely under an overpaint of ochre, black, and white. This new color was scraped off with the painting knife, chiefly in the distance. Such a procedure always leaves some of the paint imbedded in the surface of the underpainting; this creates a different texture from

**Figure 65A** Underpainting: light gray (umber, Prussian blue, white). Glaze: Prussian blue, umber, ochre. Scumble into the wet glaze: white, applied with the painting knife.

**65B** Instead of the glaze, the paint was solid, mixed with white. The light effects were produced with the scriptliner on the top part, and with the striper on the bottom part of the picture.

65A

65B

128

**Figure 66A**  The bluish gray underpainting was glazed with Prussian blue, ochre, and umber; the lower part was scumbled with white.

**Figure 66B**  The same glaze was spread over the lower part of the surface, and then scraped off in places with the knife, leaving a distinct texture. The upper part shows darker brush marks.

**66A**

**66B**

**67A**

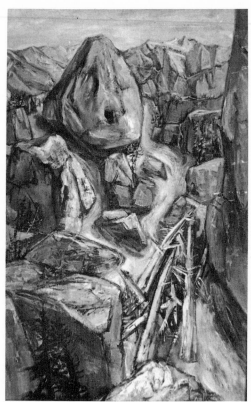

◄Figure 67A *The Waterfall* (24″ x 32″). With the exception of draftsman-like effects (for which the scriptliner is the ideal instrument, in landscape painting), the entire picture was done with the knife—or, I should rather say, a variety of knives, because an appropriate blade must be used for a particular occasion. The difficulty in this painting was handling the transition of rock and water. This was solved by a simple procedure: the water area was glazed with Prussian blue, umber, and white (on a light gray underpainting); into the wet glaze, white was scumbled over the entire surface. Next day, when this was dry, another glaze, mixed from the same colors but appreciably darker, was applied to the water areas that are in shade. Into this wet glaze, scumbling with white—in a few places—suggests the white foam of the rushing water.

Figure 67B    Detail of rocks and water. ▼

Figure 67C    Detail of trees and water in lower right. ▼

Figure 67D    Detail of brush and knife treatment in fallen trees and rocks. ▶

**67B**

**67C**

Figure 68A *The Island* (28″ x 38″).
Like *The Waterfall,* this painting
was finished almost entirely with
the knife. The light area of the
water is opaque, and its color
corresponds to that of the sky: it
is dull pink, with greenish and
grayish overtones (white, Naples
yellow, Venetian red, viridian
green). The dark area (lower part
of the picture) is all in glazes:
Prussian blue and umber. The
underpainting for the entire water
area was light gray.

Figure 68B   Detail of *The Island.*

those shown in preceding examples.

Only very few colors were mentioned for painting water: Prussian blue, viridian green, ochre, and umber, in addition to black and white. A few more will be needed at times. For yellowish nuances, we could use ochre or Naples yellow with white; by adding a little Venetian red, we would obtain a useful pink. But, at times, water could be a strong green, in which case cadmium yellow would have to be added to the mixture with Prussian blue and/or black. Why I can only think of Prussian blue for water effects may be due to a personal predilection. But, leaving all idiosyncracies of taste aside, no other blue except phthalo has sufficient tinting power to maneuver other colors into their proper position with ease.

Other examples of paintings where the water motifs play a major role are seen in Figs. 67 and 68.

## FURTHER OBSERVATIONS

After what has been said about landscape painting, it might appear that there is only one season—summer. Reference was made to flamboyant autumn, but the discussion was not encouraging at all. Then there is spring, of course, offering alluring possibilities—delicate colors, trees still showing their skeletal structure, twigs sprouting fresh greens—surely landscapes of enchantment.

And how about winter? Here, we step again on treacherous ground! I must confess that I have been traumatized by a winter scene, a picture which has haunted me since my childhood: Brueghel's *Hunters in Snow*. Whenever I have thought of painting winter, that picture has come to my mind and infected me with diffidence! For me, it contains everything one could ever wish to express about winter. Hence, only on the rarest occasions do I dare tackle the subject and, when I do, echoes of Brueghel's winter mood furtively intrude upon the scene.

But these are purely personal difficulties. Putting them aside, we may look back in history to seek aid and enlightenment. How were winter landscapes treated in the past? The Netherlandish masters (15th-17th century) did it in the most superb, incomparable manner. But they received formidable support: the style of their time. Can winter be adequately handled in a styleless age? Provided that one avoids the sunlit snow (yellowish in light, purple in shade) as we see it on the calendar picture, winter landscapes can be done. Hence, one would have to avoid such blatant coloring, as well as the heavy blanket of snow, and treat snowy effects with great discretion.

Instructions like those in this chapter may seem to have constricting finality. However, when you deal with things that can be rendered pictorially, there *are* many ways of representing them—good ways and ways that are not so good. It is my contention that the instructions given on these pages—though not covering all possible solutions—are bound to lead to good results. With practice, the results will be worth your effort.

# CHAPTER 12

# *The art of landscape painting*

In recapturing the world around him, the artist can go about it with his eyes closed, as it were, or he can fix his gaze on a specific vista with the relentless eye of a camera lens. His repertoire may be limited to his own backyard, or he may submerge himself in distant and foreign climes. Whether he reproduces or invents, he creates a new world.

Whatever avenue of approach he may choose, the authenticity of his interpretation will not necessarily depend upon fidelity to his subject matter, for artistic validity transcends geographic and botanical limits. A painting of a nearby wooded park, or of the Grand Canyon, no matter how faithfully realized, will not be convincing if the artist's vision is not fed by a fertile imagination. However, the artist does not necessarily show imagination when he invents or dramatizes his themes; the most humble object can be visualized realistically, and its image can be profound and significant. With practice and concentration, you can develop the faculties of seeing and rendering in a creative, imaginative fashion. You will find this practice well worth the effort.

## GATHERING PICTORIAL MATERIAL

After this short introduction, you may ask yourselves, how should we go about composing a landscape? What scenes should we choose? Should we paint what catches our attention on the spot or assemble the motifs according to our own ideas? Should we work from previously made sketches and notes, or from photos, prints, or what have you?

These are legitimate questions: to answer them we shall have to get advice from our teachers—the masters of the past. It was the Flemish painters of the 15th century who started painting landscapes for their own sake, in which the human presence is usually unimportant. Of course, landscape motifs appeared at the same time in Germany and Italy, although here the accent on figures was more pronounced.

During the 15th and later centuries, and up to the time of the Barbizon School (the name is derived from a village near Fontainebleau, France, where a group of painters settled during the mid-19th century), landscape painting was done in the studio, not in the open. However, natural forms were studied in numerous drawings. Some of these drawings (often translated into etchings and engravings), like those by Dürer, show encyclopedic knowledge of the anatomy of landscape motifs. But no artist, before the 19th century, ever planted his easel in the open and started to wield a brush on the spur of the moment.

Considering the involved technical procedures (all previously discussed in this book), such attempts would have been virtually impossible. And what about the Barbizon School and the Impressionists, who were of a later generation? The Barbizon painters still, in a fashion, observed many classic precepts when they dealt with landscape motifs and their illumination was invariably *studio light*. The Impressionists, although they did attempt to paint out in the open—directly on white canvas without underpainting—like the painters before them, they nearly always made changes once the canvas was moved into the studio.

These innovators always worked in plein air (light found in the open). They would face their motifs squarely—let us say, a haystack (a favorite object with Monet)—and paint it at 10 A.M., 12 Noon, 2 P.M., and so forth, capturing the different effects of light and shade. Also, regarding composition, they would never dare to change what met their eyes, for the cry of the day was "be true to nature." Well, as always, returning to nature can mean many things to many men.

Thus, it appears that painting can be done directly from nature, but because the techniques described in this book are not adapted to such practices (except in alla prima painting), this direct approach shall not be discussed here. Then again, a composition can be planned according to one's own ideas; we may consult our imagination or our sketchbook; we may even gather facts from a photo or a number of photos. These, in my opinion, should be black and white, for colors in photos are always misleading—as far as our purpose is concerned.

Now I can see some raised eyebrows. Using photos? It is legitimate? Can a painting made from a photo be considered "original?" We could ask further: from where do we derive

such standards of "professional ethics?" Why should a work done from a three-dimensional "sample" (as in nature) attest to a painter's honesty, while a work done from a two-dimensional sample (photo) is "wrong?" The plain truth is that one can be more of a copyist working directly from nature than from the imagination or from an ordinary photograph. It all depends on how the artist conceives his picture.

## CLASSIC PRINCIPLES OF LANDSCAPE CONSTRUCTION

Here is a step-by-step analysis of the classical method of executing a landscape in colors.

1. Draw the composition on paper first, and save it for future reference.

2. Transfer the drawing to the white canvas.

3. Finish one or more underpaintings with the knife.

4. Reestablish and improve the drawing, which has become largely obliterated by the underpainting.

5. Oil the canvas, or as much of it as you expect to paint in one session.

6. Start to paint *the farthermost distance*. Now the farthermost distance is, of course, the sky. But the sky is not always the first to be finished. Just as in portrait painting the background is the last to be done, so the final appearance of the sky cannot be previsualized with certainty. When painting a portrait, for example, the color of the background must be adjusted to the general color scheme of the picture, the lighting, the expression of the model—and not the other way around. The sky, too, will often reflect the mood of the landscape, and the colors of the ground area will influence the appearance of the sky.

But when objects in front of the sky form complicated silhouettes, it will be impossible to paint the sky around them (that is, when you follow the classic technique). If this is the case, the sky shall have to occupy us first, though its color, applied before we paint the ground area, will be an approximation. The principal color areas can be modified later, as required.

7. The logic of the procedure established in the paragraph above will continue throughout the

Figure 69 The order of painting
a landscape, in classic technique:
begin with the furthermost distance
and progress, in stages, to the
motifs in the foreground.

entire working period: the most distant planes first, next, the adjoining areas nearer to us, and so forth. The last surface to be painted is the one in the forefront. This system is graphically represented in Fig. 69.

### DEMONSTRATION OF CLASSIC TECHNIQUE: UNDERPAINTING

All paintings introduced on the preceding pages (except those in the demonstrations) were done some time ago. The last example, *The Rising Moon* (Fig. 70), was painted "live," so to speak, to give the reader a step-by-step account of its development. Hence, photos of its early stages are introduced here.

The first underpainting (not reproduced) proved to be unsatisfactory; the color of the sky was too light. This lightness would have made the planned glaze on top of it too active. The paint in the background and middleground (yellowish gray) was too thin, and the foreground required a much stronger (smooth) impasto. Hence a second underpainting had to be applied (Fig. 70A).

On this underpainting, one characteristic should be noted: the lack of details. Only the principal masses are differentiated: the sky, the expanse of ground, and the mass of rock in the foreground. Without the charcoal drawing, which appears here in sketchy form, the composition would have remained fairly inarticulate.

As to the drawing, the first underpainting largely obliterated it. Another sketch was developed on top of the first underpainting. This, in turn, almost disappeared after the second underpainting was applied. After it dried, the third drawing—an improved version —was again done in charcoal, and it was made indelible with fixative.

Because the composition was first drawn on paper, it was possible to refer to the original plan throughout the working period. As you can realize from the above, the intermediate stages of work allowed the initial idea to steadily improve and mature. Although one of the important principles of underpainting is to blur the contours, in this particular landscape the

**Figure 70A** *Rising Moon* (26″
x 36″). Second underpainting.
Sky: phthalo blue and white.
Moon: Naples yellow, Venetian red,
white. Ground: Mars yellow, dark
ochre, white. Foreground: umber,
burnt siena, white.

blending was not carried out to any great extent. (Actually, the transitions, now obscured by the charcoal marks, are softer than they appear on the reproduction.)

In Fig. 70A, the second underpainting was carried out using the following colors: on the sky area, phthalo blue and white were applied with the blending knife, in a layer so thin that the orange from within became faintly visible. The moon received its final color, which was not to be overpainted: a yellow-pink mixed from Naples yellow, a little Venetian red, and white. A brown-yellow (Mars yellow, dark ochre, and white) was applied to the ground area. The mass of rocks in the foreground was painted in a smooth but appreciable impasto, with umber, burnt siena, and white.

When we examine the general underpainting of the picture, it becomes clear that no special underpainting was provided for the trees or for the rather complex rock formations in the middleground. The reason for this is twofold. First, small details do not need a particular underpainting when the pictorial conception is not miniaturistic. Secondly, it is obvious that the absence of such underpaintings allows improvisation because we are not compelled to follow a prearranged scheme, but may obey a momentary impulse and thus gain greater freedom. As for the trees, they belong to the foreground, hence they were the last ones to be treated.

## DEMONSTRATION OF CLASSIC TECHNIQUE: FINAL PAINTING

In Fig. 70B, an intermediate stage of painting can be see. The sky was painted thinly with a glaze of viridian green, Prussian blue, white, and a little umber. The same colors, rendered opaque with some Venetian red added, were used for the clouds. Naples yellow was scumbled over most of the area around the moon. At this stage, the sky appears finished and the moon still remains hidden beneath the color of the sky. When painting the sky, it would have been foolish to do it around the moon. Hence, in this instance, the moon was overpainted, and then the color was wiped off with a piece of cheesecloth.

Next, to unify the tonality of the ground area, a glaze of zinc yellow and black was spread over the entire surface. The details as they appear in the middleground, were painted into this wet glaze. Neither the water, the foreground, nor the trees were considered as yet.

The color of the water area, at this point still uncertain, will have to be harmonized with the final color of the ground, and the motifs in front will be the last ones treated. These adjustments made, the medium-sized canvas was finished in a day's work; hence the trunks of the trees and the foliage were painted at the very end, into a surface that was still wet.

# CHAPTER 13

# *Varnishing*

Why should one varnish paintings? There are two main reasons: to reestablish the value and depth of colors as they appeared when still wet, and to protect the paint surface.

In time, colors tend to become lusterless and dull, even to the point of losing their identity. This invariably happens when, during the drying process, the medium and/or the binder becomes absorbed by the lower strata of paint. Also, paint with low oil content tends to dry without gloss. Such paint is porous and therefore subject to decay because its linoxyn is weak. A porous linoxyn surface attracts dirt, and once dirt becomes incorporated in the paint film, its removal can become quite problematic. Moisture, too, acts adversely upon this kind of a surface.

A flat, oil-starved surface also has another weakness: in time, it becomes powdery because of the insufficient bond between the oil and the pigment particles. Should this occur, the use of resin varnish would not be a proper remedy; more about this when we discuss the process of varnishing.

## HOW VARNISH PROTECTS PAINTINGS

Varnish safeguards the permanence of the painting by forming a cohesive film which protects the surface from dirt. The slick varnish film can be easily dusted, and when it eventually becomes soiled by atmospheric impurities (tobacco smoke, kitchen fumes, soot, etc.), the varnish can be easily removed without injury to the paint film.

Moreover, varnish tends to prevent penetration of moisture, one of the contributing factors to the decay of the paint surface, along with extreme levels of temperature and atmospheric humidity.

I said that the varnish can be easily removed without injury to the paint film—but this is not always true. If the paint was diluted by a medium containing a sufficient quantity of damar or mastic (the soft resins), any solvent capable of removing the varnish would inevitably attack the paint film. The glazed parts are especially vulnerable when the picture is cleaned.

## RECOMMENDED VARNISHES

First, what kind of varnishes should be used? There are three principal kinds: *retouching varnish, damar picture varnish,* and *copal varnish.* Because these varnishes do not behave uniformly—the formulas are not identical with all the manufacturers—I am referring here to compounds produced by Permanent Pigments from my own formulations.

*Retouching varnish* (so-called for want of a better designation), is the *lightest* of the three because it has the least concentration of resin. It can be used on relatively fresh paintings—ones that have dried for about two weeks. However, the paint, at this early stage, is still quite vulnerable; therefore, the varnish should be applied sparingly with a soft brush, *without* undue pressure or rubbing. The painting should be covered sparingly with varnish. Spraying varnish from a pressure can (common when using fixative on drawings) is totally inappropriate.

*Damar picture varnish* is differently formulated; it serves to protect well-dried paintings. When can a painting be considered thoroughly dry? This again depends entirely on the condition of the paint layers. A *normally* thick paint stratum—one or two thin underpaintings with one or two thin overpaints—may need a year to be considered sufficiently dry, although the actual drying (that is the oxidation process) will continue for a great many years.

Damar picture varnish can be applied with any brush, but long, elastic bristles are best. After you brush it on, the wet varnish can be rubbed in with the side of your hand, thus producing a uniformily thin film. Whereas retouching varnish becomes completely dry to the touch in a short while, the very slight tackiness of damar picture varnish will last for a day or two. Under normal conditions, a varnished, well-dried painting will not require revarnishing for twenty-five years—a conservative figure.

And now to *copal varnish.* How does it differ from the damar preparations? Copal has the best lasting quality; therefore, it should be used on paintings several years old, although it may replace the damar picture varnish. Contrary to some reports found in obsolete manuals, a properly formulated copal product has all the su-

perior properties we can expect of a varnish. When used on older paintings, it can be applied with a piece of cheesecloth, which is ideal for varnishing larger surfaces, although its hard nap (or hard rubbing) could injure surfaces that have solidified completely.

Lastly, there is *Matte Picture Varnish* (Permanent Pigments) which I formulated especially for those who prefer a semi-matte picture surface. This varnish can be used shortly after a painting has been finished. Polishing the dry, varnished surface can produce a gloss without impairing the protective quality of the product.

The opinion sometimes voiced, that premature varnishing damages a painting's permanence is, to all intents and purposes, without substantiation. In fact, it is the *varnish,* not the paint, which suffers on a surface that has not had time to solidify well. Fresh, or relatively fresh paint layers will, in time, destroy the cohesion of a varnish; therefore, fresh paintings may require repeated varnishing. After a few months, the surface may become dull again in spots and require revarnishing; it all depends on the condition of the paint strata—a thick layer of paint will need a much longer time to dry. The varnish may disappear from such a surface, even after a year or two.

To reveal its true color, an oil painting cannot be perfectly flat—that is, non-glossy—unless it is painted entirely in light colors, or is, to begin with, chalky in tone. Flat (or matte) paintings are usually done on absorbent primings and, therefore, cannot be successfully varnished, for a varnish will not form a cohesive film on such surfaces. However, when a painting is too glossy, this can be quite disturbing. When they face a window, such paintings, especially when they are dark, reflect light like a mirror. In such instances, Matte Picture Varnish can be helpful in reducing the gloss.

## MISCELLANEOUS COMMENTS ON VARNISHING

As I mentioned, the best brush to use for varnishing is a soft bristle brush, or even a small utility brush, providing the bristles are long and soft. If the body of the bristles is too thick (which impairs elasticity), it should be reduced by cutting off some of the bristles, at the neck of the ferrule, with a razor blade.

While it is being varnished, the painting should be held horizontally toward the light so that you may see and control the spreading of the varnish and the forming of the glossy film.

When still fresh, differently textured areas of a painting may differ in their degree of gloss. In certain instances, it may take a long time before the varnish can produce a uniform gloss. Sometimes small areas of the surface will remain flat even after several varnish applications. This will indicate that a break in the underlying film absorbed the oil from the paint, leaving the particular spot oil-starved. The only remedy here is to *oil the spots or the areas* with the copal painting medium. This will prevent the paint stratum from becoming powdery. Although this works well on relatively fresh paintings, such a remedy is not always complete because the oily medium does not penetrate a well-dried surface thoroughly.

Sometimes the varnish will trickle; there is no satisfactory explanation for this occurrence. However, gentle rubbing of the varnished surface with the side of the hand, using circular motions, will, in the end, produce the desired results.

It is good practice to varnish a picture methodically, proceeding from top to bottom, and to treat a surface only about one square foot at a time.

If a painting requires cleaning before revarnishing, it should be done in the following manner. First, dust the surface with a soft cloth. Next, rub the paint with your fingers; it is amazing how much dirt will come off a surface which seems clean. The removal of the old varnish will be the next step. This can be done with a wad of surgical cotton dipped in a mild solvent such as mineral spirits (sold under various trade names like Sunoco Spirits, Texaco Spirits, Varnolene, and Painters' Thinner). Should the solvent penetrate the reverse side of the canvas (which happens when the paint film is not solid enough or if it has minute openings), delay the varnishing for at least a day. It is important to allow the solvent to evaporate before you attempt the revarnishing. A fabric which absorbs the diluent dries quite slowly; if you varnish a picture during the drying process, the evaporating solvent would destroy the fresh varnish, leaving a blotchy surface.

Now, perhaps the painting has been varnished, but it appears desirable to make corrections at this stage. The usual procedure is to start by rubbing the painting medium onto the surface of the picture. But, in this case, the soft varnish would incorporate itself into the medium, which is not desirable. Therefore, the surface to be overpainted should be freed from the varnish by using a wad of surgical cotton dipped in turpentine or one of the previously mentioned petrol solvents. Then, you can rub the painting medium onto the surface and commence to repaint.

If copal varnish was used on the painting, the painting medium can be rubbed into it; but, in this case, the medium's viscosity will increase considerably. This is not necessarily a disadvantage. It all depends on your working method; in many cases, painting into a viscous surface is very agreeable.

# CHAPTER 14

# *Analyses of landscape paintings*

"Good judgment comes from good understanding, and good understanding comes from principles derived from good rules, and good rules are the daughters of good experience, the common mother of all sciences and arts." Implicit in these simple words of Albrecht Dürer is the wisdom that should guide the painter: seek counsel with the great masters of the past.

## STUDYING OLD MASTERS

Now, the contemporary landscape painter may ask, "Why should I look back to the past? Is not 'originality' the password of the day?" We may answer with another quotation by the great art historian, Max J. Friedländer: "Powerful artists have at all times wrestled with nature and acquired a style, each man his own. In the twentieth century, they fight for style, with mannerism as the result." To which we may add: originality of expression can never be attained by neglect of tradition. For originality does not imply that tradition has been cast aside, but that it has been developed and enlarged. In the history of art, we see again and again that true originality is greatest where indebtedness to the past is strongest.

To demonstrate the development of classic landscape painting in a few significant examples, a chronological order has been maintained, beginning with the work of Carpaccio and ending with the 19th century painters, Cézanne and Van Gogh.

Figure 71 Vittore Carpaccio (1450?–1523?), *Meditation on the Passion,* Metropolitan Museum of Art. As the landscape is an accessory to the figures, it could have been omitted without leaving holes in the ensemble. This work belongs with some of the most remarkable early Venetian art because of its grandiose composition and the delicacy of the details which, like all minutiae in Gothic and early Renaissance painting, form self-sufficient, complete units, independent of their surroundings. While this is an archaic manner of visualization, it need not be considered antiquated. The difficulty of using such conceptions adequately, however, lies in the incident of style—the authentic expression of a certain age. To make it authentic in our time, an overtone of Surrealism— or we may call it an element of ambiguity—would have to enter the picture.

Figure 71B Detail of *Meditation on the Passion.* ▶

**Figure 72A** Lucas Cranach (1472–1553), *The Judgment of Paris,* Metropolitan Museum of Art. Here, too, figures dominate the scene, but the landscape motif, one could rightly say, is of greater importance. In fact, the slightly ludicrous actors of the *Judgment* seem to be an excuse for the artist's preoccupation with the landscape. The style of the painting is unmistakably German, with a strong influence from the Flemish school. All details, regardless of their position in space, are seen in sharp focus; but they are not as subtle as those seen in Carpaccio's work, discussed earlier. The technique of the painting is identical with that used by the Flemish masters almost a century earlier. It is interesting to observe how the trees were painted. Here the design of the foliage was, we may say, incised with light, extra long paint into the solid, viscous layer of dark green.

**Figure 72B** Detail of *The Judgment of Paris.*

Figure 73A   Joachim Patinir (1480?–1524), *St. Jerome*, National Gallery, London. One of the first landscape painters, this Flemish master was so disinterested in figures that when these were not in miniature, he entrusted them to his colleague, preferably the illustrious Quentin Massys. The sky area in this painting occupies only one fifth of the picture, thus giving the painter an opportunity to utilize immense vistas of the landscape and register its manifold activities. It is obvious that such details as the saint and other figures, as well as the dwellings, were a concession which Patinir made to the picture-buying public; thus he justified his exclusive preoccupation with landscape. Fantastic rock formations were, as we realize from all his landscapes, his favorite themes. I may state candidly here that my own conception of landscapes and their technical management comes directly from Patinir, or to put it more inclusively, from the early Flemish school.

Figure 73B   Detail of *St. Jerome.* ▶

Figure 74A  El Greco (1541–1614), *View of Toledo,* Metropolitan Museum of Art. Considering its unconventional conception, this 16th century work has all the characteristics of a modern painting. It was executed with powerful brushstrokes, obviously El Greco was unconcerned with the rendition of fine details. The painter's interest lay in the dramatic aspect of the scenery. And this effect was produced in the first place by the lighting, which we may call illogical, or more correctly, expressionistic, because it does not conform systematically to the rules of ordered chiaroscuro—that is, a focal light that issues from one source only.

It is interesting to observe how summarily El Greco dealt with details he considered nonessential, such as the foliage of the trees. Only the group of trees in the left corner shows some clearly differentiated foliage. The color of all these greens is obviously derived from black mixed with yellow; adding white to this mixture, the painter was able to produce a large range of subtle gray-greens. These tones were thinly painted over a ground carrying the traditional Venetian reddish color. The presence of this red ground is felt in all parts of the surface, except in the light areas which, in contrast, are treated in relative impasti. It appears that the brushes used in this painting were not in "good shape"; the bristles had a tendency to spread, a great advantage for painting loosely. You should keep in mind that a perfect brush might not be the best one when you want to achieve looseness, rather than precision, in your brushstrokes.

Figure 74B  Detail of townscape.

**Figure 74C** The diagram of the composition gives us a clue as to its structure. Such diagrams are very useful as preliminary studies when you compose a picture. Hence, when you deal with a more complex design, it is always advisable to start with a geometric pattern first. When this is worked out satisfactorily, you can then put the individual motifs in their respective places.

**Figure 74D** Detail of river and bridge.

Figure 75A  Pieter Brueghel (1525?–1569), *The Harvesters,* Metropolitan Museum of Art. This large panel was painted alla prima on a light ochre imprimatura in glazes, and, in some places, semi-glazes. Only the greens of the trees' foliage are opaque; these show relative impasti—and there can be no doubt that a hard resin medium must have been used for the dilution of paint. As usual, in all areas where the foliage appears as a compact mass, the dark color was applied first, and the definition of leaves in full light was made into the wet, dark paint. The alla prima technique described earlier in this treatise differs in no way from that used by 16th century painters. As in all Flemish paintings of that era, the horizon line is high up on the picture plane, although not as high as was common a century earlier.

◀Figure 75B Detail of *The Harvesters.*

Figure 75C Diagram of the structure of the composition. In the *Harvesters,* the vertical division marked by the tree in the foreground is arranged according to the golden section. The distant planes roll off into space, winding and interwinding in curves, straight lines, and serpentines. All forms are held together by the molded sweep of the wheatfield, which cuts obliquely across the foreground. Here the master strategist anchored the dark mass of the foliage into the vertical axis of the picture. Thus, the eye never leaves the scene it is engaged in exploring. ▶

75C

▼Figure 75D Detail of *The Harvesters.*

Figure 76    Jan Van Goyen (1596–1656), *View of Haarlem,* Metropolitan Museum of Art. This painting and Fig. 77, are typical examples of 17th century Dutch landscape painting, where human presence is incidental. Here, the tiny figures found occasionally seem to have one purpose only: to introduce a speck of red into the mass of lush green. The art of pure landscape painting flourished in Northern countries rather than in Italy, where landscape motifs were a mere foil for compositions with figures.

In the *View of Haarlem,* the expanse of sky reverses the proportion seen on the Patinir pictures; here we note that the area of the land covers one fifth of the entire surface. This painting is a splendid example of alla prima painting on toned ground; all the virtues of this technique are realized here. Swift movements of the sable brush, without amendments or changes, inscribe tiny details on the picture's surface in a calligraphic manner. There is interplay between the lambent light and shade, as in most of the

Dutch landscapes of this era. The illumination is provided by the radiant sky and its swiftly moving clouds. These clouds, in some places, obscure the flatlands and, in others, allow the light to bring them into brilliant focus. Such devices of illumination were not new; many of the Italian Baroque painters used them a century earlier. The great charm of the *View of Haarlem* rests also, to a large degree, in the ribbon-like parallel segments of the distant, interchanging land and water areas.

Figure 77 Meindert Hobbema
(1638–1709), *A Woodland Road*,
Metropolitan Museum of Art.
In this painting, the luminous
sky contrasts dramatically with
the dark, ragged woodland.
Technically, this picture is not
outstanding; its attraction rests
chiefly in the particular lighting
and composition that distinguishes
the 17th century Dutch school.

**Figure 78 Philips de Koninck (1619–1688),** *Landscape,* Metropolitan Museum of Art. Both this painting and Fig. 79 show the most effective arrangements of light and shade patterns caused by billowing clouds. They cast their shadows on the ground, in some places, or, in other areas, allow shafts of brilliant light to play over the surface of the earth. This very large landscape is a masterpiece of pictorial understatement; no particular object is given the task of catching the beholder's attention.

The typically Dutch countryside unrolls itself in flat ribbons, embellished by small, inconspicuous details. Their parallel arrangement is countered only by the serpentine movement of the elevated foreground, which, with its brilliantly lighted surface, arrests our attention before guiding us persuasively into the infinite distance. At the sides, small hills guard the distant, gleaming stretches and do not allow the land and the waterways to run beyond the picture's frame.

**Figure 79** Jacob van Ruisdael (1628–1682), *Wheatfields,* Metropolitan Museum of Art. True to the prevailing style, the sky occupies the major area; its radiant quality endows the tracts of wheatfields with a golden aura. This illumination and the keen foreshortening of the foreground's recessive furrows (seen from what we have called a worm's eye view) lead the beholder magically into the dense, soft green of the woods; here our attention, framed by the luminescent segments of the wheatfield, rests in enchantment.

**Figure 80**   Francesco Guardi
(1712–1793), *Fantastic Landscape,*
Metropolitan Museum of Art.
Guardi's large decorative landscape
was done alla prima on a toned
priming of light gray in the upper
part, and on a yellowish priming
under the predominantly shadowy
foreground. With the exception of
the sky area, the entire surface is
painted in glazes of varying density.
Such a technique and the sketchy
treatment of details allowed the
painter to finish this 61″ x 74″
canvas in a very short time—
perhaps in two days or less.

Figure 81  Bernardo Bellotto (1724–1780), *View of Vaprio d'Adda*, Metropolitan Museum of Art. Bellotto's landscape, although it derives its style from the same source as does Guardi (Venetian Rococo), is not painted alla prima; its technique aims at a pedantic elaboration of details. The swift staccato strokes of the scriptliner, so common in almost all of Guardi's paintings, are used here only to indicate the rippled surface of the river. Wherein lies the compelling attraction of these paintings—aside from the intrinsic charm of the Venetian Rococo style? It lies in the light of the declining sun—the improviser of nostalgic moods. If used judiciously and tactfully, this light can become the painter's most eloquent instrument of persuasion.

## 19TH CENTURY PAINTINGS

The 19th century paintings illustrate the schism between the classic and the nonclassic approach to things pictorial. This is of interest because it demonstrates the interdependence of painting techniques and esthetic theories. It is obvious that only a certain pictorial idiom can adequately express a particular pictorial idea. Of course, the 19th century did create an accurate division between the classic and the nonclassic, for styles always overlap and cannot be limited to definite time periods. During the first half of the 19th century, the echoes of the classic mode were still alive. Ingres was born in 1780, Goya died in 1828, and Delacroix, who should be considered the last exponent of the classic tradition, lived until 1863.

All the significant art movements that shaped the representational art of our time ended at the beginning of this century. It must also be recognized that, although few of these movements became really significant, they served well as sources that still generate new ideas still in use today.

Figure 82 Vincent Van Gogh (1853–1890), *The Starry Night,* Museum of Modern Art. Van Gogh's paintings belong to the category of Post-impressionism. Coloristically, they are part impressionistic and part expressionistic. Now, in the words of Roger Fry, "The essential point of Expressionism is that the artist tries not only to realize his idea, but to express to the world his feeling about his idea." Not only is Van Gogh's color (in pictures like the *Starry Night*) emotionally conditioned, but his forms are also highly agitated. What is an emotionally conditioned color? It is one chosen according to the painter's feelings, rather than dictated by the actual appearance of the motif. Hence, in such a system, a sky may appear red; water, a sulphur yellow, and so on.

Figure 82B Vincent Van Gogh, *Cypresses,* Metropolitan Museum of Art. All of Van Gogh's paintings are painted in heavy impasti done alla prima, and organized in undulating rhythmic sequences. Entirely original, his technique has never been successfully used by any other painter. Van Gogh was one of the few who painted directly from nature, no matter how much he deviated from the actual image. He used his paints as they came from the tubes, undiluted by any medium, employing bristle brushes only. Once a painting was finished, it was seldom, if ever, retouched. It is little known that, working in this manner, he was able to accomplish several paintings in a few hours—on good days.

Figure 82C  Details of *Cypresses.*

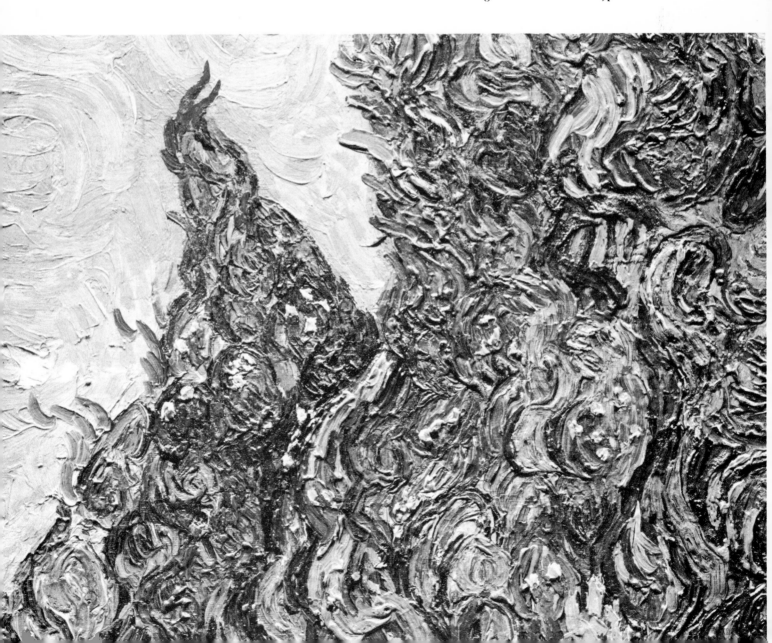

Figure 83A Paul Cézanne (1839–1906), *The Seine Near Paris,* Museum of Art, Rhode Island School of Design. Leaving aside all the mythology that has been woven around this painter's work, the characteristics of his technique and pictorial conceptions are as follows. His later painting was always done from nature, alla prima. Colors were applied thinly with bristle brushes to the white canvas, which often remained uncovered in many places.

In what respect does his approach differ from that of the Impressionists? First, he abandoned aerial perspective: colors do not lose their value progressively; the same set of colors may appear in the middleground and foreground. Such paintings have what is known as an *equalized* surface. The infinite distance is never seen in his paintings, and linear perspective is not arranged in a funnel-like manner, but is arrested in the middle of the picture—stopped by a motif that does not allow the eye to move to the horizon line. Thus, recessions in his paintings rely on intersection and overlapping of planes (Fig. 33B).

Further, the use of a multiple viewpoint (see Fig. 37E) is another perspective device found in some of his paintings, in addition to a ruthless sacrifice of all details not essential to form. This allowed him to concentrate on pure structure, which led, in the end, to his (unintentional) invention of Cubism. Contrary to impressionistic dabs, dots, and daubs, Cézanne occasionally used diagonal brushstrokes moving from right to left over the entire surface; more often, however, the brush marks appear as flat patches. Although, officially, he is looked upon as a master colorist, this is demonstrably false. Cézanne's characteristic work is painted in monotones. Because form and color compete, a painter who stresses the *structural* can therefore not rely on polychromatic effects, without detracting from the form.

Figure 83B Detail of *The Seine Near Paris* ▶

# Glossary

*Alla prima:* painting without underpainting.

*Configuration of paint:* the plastic appearance of a paint surface.

*Gel:* jellylike substance.

*Gesso:* white pigment bound by size.

*Glaze:* a darker, transparent color film applied to a lighter underpainting.

*Hiding power:* the degree of opacity in paint.

*Hygroscopic:* having the capacity to absorb water.

*Impasto:* a thick application of paint.

*Imprimatura:* a glaze applied to a primed support before painting.

*Linoxyn:* dried paint film.

*Long paint:* paint which does not retain brushstrokes but seeks a level.

*Pigment:* dry color matter.

*Polymerization:* changes in molecular grouping of certain liquids.

*Priming:* a surface applied to a support prior to painting.

*Resin:* exudates of certain coniferous trees.

*Resin, hard:* exudate from trees now extinct.

*Resin, soft:* exudate from living trees.

*Rosin:* a residue left after distillation of turpentine.

*Scumble:* a semi-transparent application of light paint to a darker underpainting.

*Short paint:* paint which, when heaped up, retains a sharp configuration.

*Siccative:* a liquid used for speeding up, the drying of paint.

*Stabilizers:* materials used to keep pigment and oil in suspension.

*Tooth:* roughness or graininess of a surface.

*Varnish:* a solution of resin in a diluent.

*Vehicle:* a binder for pigments.

*Viscosity:* relative capacity of a liquid to flow.

# Index

Alberti, Leon Battista, 59

Alla prima painting, 26, 29, 80, 82–94, 97, 136, 155, 157, 162, 163, 167; characteristics of, 83; history of, 82–83; on toned ground, 89

Background, 58, 63–64

Bacon, Roger, 59

Balance, 43; color, 64–66

Barbizon School, 135, 136

Bellotto, Bernardo, illus. by, 161

Bosch, Hiernonymus, 82, 93, 98

Bristle brushes, 15–17, 29, 107, 112, 120, 167, 168; cleaning, 21; for painting sky, 101; for scumbling, 81; for underpainting, 96; for varnishing, 142–143

Brueghel, Pieter, 19, 134; illus. by, 153, 154, 155

Brushes, 15–22; bristle, 15–17, 29, 81, 97, 101, 107, 112, 120, 144–145, 167, 168; caring for, 21–22; flat sable, 17; round sable, 17–18, 26, 54, 83, 91, 101, 102, 112, 118, 120, 158; sabeline, 17; scriptliner, 18–20, 39, 40, 41, 54, 83, 85, 86, 91, 108, 111, 114, 118, 119, 123, 127, 128, 130, 163; striper, 20, 114, 119, 123, 128; illus. of, 16, 17, 18

Canaletto, 18

Canvas, 25–29 *passim*, 78; comparing, 25–27; for alla prima painting, 82; preparing, 27–28; illus. of, 26

Carborundum paper, 89

Carpaccio, Vittore, 146, 149, 150; illus. by, 147

Cézanne, Paul, 59, 63, 97, 144; illus. by, 168, 169

Charcoal, 29, 83

Chiaroscuro, 153

Clouds, color of, 73–74

Coherence, 50

Colors, 30–34; body, 31, 34, 70, 98; characteristics of, 34; cold, 30; complementary, 71, 98; closed, 92; in underpainting, 98; local, 33; mixing, 70–76; of clouds, 73–74; of horizon, 74; of rocks, 75; of sky, 73; of trees, 75; of water, 75–76; on the palette, 72; opaque, 32, 34, 77; open, 92; transparent, 77; warm, 30

Composition, 42–57; and picture format, 66–68; balance in, 43; coherence, unity, emphasis in, 48–50; nature of, 43–48; problems of, 42–43; strategy of, 48; vs. design, 43

Cranach, Lucas, illus. by, 148

Crawling, *see* Trickling

Crayon, 83
Cubism, 166

Da Vinci, Leonardo, 59
De Koninck, Philips, illus. by, 160
Delacroix, Eugene, 98, 164
Details, 137
Diluents, 35–41; function of, 36–37
Doerner, Max, 37, 80
Drier, cobalt, 41
Dürer, Albrecht, 59, 136, 146

El Greco, 98; illus. by, 152, 153, 154
Emphasis, 50
Equipment, 15–24, 25–29
Euclid, 59

Ferrule, 16, 21
Fixative, 29, 83, 85, 90
Focus, 63–64
Foreground, 58, 63–64, 74
Forest, 112–118
Francesco, Piero della, 59
Friedländer, Max J., 146
Fry, Roger, 165

Gel, 27
Gesso, 78, 83, 85; acrylic, 28
Glaze, 77–81 passim; 91, 155, 162; see also Glazing
Glazing, 34, 36, 71, 74, 83, 84–85, 88, 106, 118, 120, 125, 127, 128, 129; over foliage, 111 see also Glaze
Golden section, 57
Goya, Francisco, 98, 164
Guardi, Francesco, 18, 98, 163; illus. by, 162
Gypsum, 28

Hals, Frans, 16, 98
Highlights, 123
Hobbema, Meindert, illus. by, 159
Horizon, color of, 74

Impasto, 23, 26, 27, 28, 40, 89–90, 96, 97, 107, 111, 112, 120, 123, 127, 140, 155, 167; for rock masses, 118
Impressionism, 69, 97, 98, 136
Imprimatura, 83–85, 88, 89, 155; multicolored, 89

India ink, 83
Ingres, J. A. D., 164

Kerosene, 21, 29

Laboratory of the Royal Museum, Brussels, 98- 99
Light, 153; focal, 69
Linseed oil, 35, 36, 90; and imprimatura, 84; for glazes, 80; thinned with turpentine, 41

Massys, Quentin, 150
Medium, Copal Painting, 18, 27, 36, 78
Mediums, see Diluents
Middleground, 58, 63–64, 74, 75
Monet, Claude, 136

Negative space, 54

Painting knives, 22–24, 36, 40, 85, 91, 102, 112, 114, 124, 125, 127, 129, 133; and alla prima technique, 83; faults of, 21; for painting sky, 101; for painting rock masses, 118; for underpainting, 96, 97; for glazing, 77; good, 22; conditioning, 23; value of, 24; illus. of, 23
Palette, 72
Palette knives, see Painting knives
Panels, 24, 25–29 passim; advantages and disadvantages of, 28–29; for alla prima painting, 82; Masonite, 29, 85; preparing, 28
Pastel, 83
Patinir, Joachim, 126, 156; illus. by, 148, 149
Pencil, 83
Percham, 59
Permanent Pigments, 41, 144
Perspective, 58–69; and focus, 63, 64; atmospheric, 64; history, 59–63
Picture format, 58–69
Polygnotus, 59
Polymerization, 35, 41
Positive space, 54
Presbyter, Theophilus, 41
Priming, 26, 27–28

Rembrandt van Rijn, 98
Resins, soft and hard, 37–41
Rocks, 100–134 passim; demonstrated, 118–126
Rubens, Peter Paul, 98

Sabeline brushes, 17

Sable brushes, 17–18, 26, 54, 83, 91, 102, 118, 158; cleaning, 21; illus. of, 17

Scriptliner brush, 18–20, 39, 40, 41, 54, 83, 85, 86, 91, 108, 111, 114, 118, 119, 123, 127, 128, 130, 163; illus. of, 20

Scumbling, 77–81, 100, 101, 107, 123, 127, 128, 130

Shade, 68

Shadow, 68

Siccative, 96

Sizing, 26, 27–28

Sky, 100–134 *passim*, 136; color of, 73; textures of, 101; underpainting for, 100

Stand oil, 36–37

Striper brush, 20, 114, 119, 123, 128; illus. of, 20

Texture, 95; of foliage, 101, 108; of skies, 101

Tiepolo, 18, 98

Tintoretto, 98

Titian, 98

Tools, 15–24 *passim*

Tracing paper, 29

Trees, 100–134 *passim;* color of, 75, 101; demonstrated, 108–118; underpainting for, 101

Trickling, 41, 90, 143

Turpentine, 21, 29, 83; for glazes, 80; to thin linseed oil, 41

Uccello, Paolo, 59

Unity, 50

Underpainting, 22–23, 26, 29, 31, 71, 78, 95–99, 100, 106, 118, 139–141, 144; color in, 98; color mixtures in, 99; for trees, 101, 106, 108; for water, 127

Van Eyck, Jan, 97, 98

Van Gogh, Vincent, 97, 146; illus. by, 165, 166, 167

Van Goyen, Jan, illus. by, 158

Van Mander, 83

Van Ruisdael, Jacob, illus. by, 161

Varnishes, 84, 127; recommended kinds of, 144

Varnishing, 37, 89, 141–145; brush for, 144–145; function of, 141

Viscosity, 34, 36

Vitellio, 59

Vitruvius, 59

Water, 100–134 *passim;* underpainting for, 127

Edited by Wilma Holden
Designed by James Craig
Composed in eleven point Baskerville by
The Haddon Craftsmen, Inc.
Printed and bound by The Haddon Craftsmen, Inc.